TEAM OF ALL THE MACS

ALAN WILSON

VERTICAL EDITIONS

www.verticaleditions.com

First published in the United Kingdom in 2011 by Vertical Editions, Unit 4a, Snaygill Industrial Estate, Skipton, North Yorkshire BD23 2QR

www.verticaleditions.com

ISBN 978–1–904091–54–7

A CIP catalogue record for this book is available from the British Library

Cover design by Harry Thornbory

Printed and bound by Jellyfish Print Solutions, Hampshire

ACKNOWLEDGEMENTS

There are a number of people, without whose help, knowledge and kindness, this book would not have been written.

Kjell Hanssen and Matt Butler both deserve huge credit for their help in spotting any mistakes in the writing and I am indebted to Harry Thornbory for the magnificent job he did on the cover design to set the tone of the book from the start. Both Karl Waddicor and Diane Evans at Vertical Editions have done a sterling job at getting this book published and without their help you would not be reading it right now.

The inspirational and undisputed authority on Merseyside football, Peter Lupson, deserves a huge pat on the back for keeping me going in bleak times as well as Peter Holme at the National Football Museum who was so incredibly generous with both his time and peerless wisdom.

Thanks also to Richard McBrearty at the Scottish Football Musuem as well as Paul Joannou and Rob Mason from the north east for kindly providing accurate information on players while I also owe a debt of gratitude to the two Stephens at Liverpool football club, Astall and Done, for their part in this project, Harry Summers for keeping the Renton dream alive, Ray Simpson at Burnley and Alastair MacLachlan at St Mirren for their specialist knowledge.

This book owes a lot to the great pioneers of

football journalism that went before me and without them recording the events all those years ago stories like this one would not be told. In particular the writers that staffed *The Field*, *Scottish Sport*, *Liverpool Echo*, *The Daily News*, *The Times* and *The Telegraph* all deserve praise, but a special thanks goes to James Catton who set the standard in football journalism for the last century thanks to his excellent *Athletic News*.

On a personal level there are many friends and, of course, my family to thank for their support. The last word, though, goes to Nailah for all her support and patience when forced to put on my football anorak without complaint. Without your help this book would never have made it off my laptop and into print so I thank you from the bottom of my heart.

To Aileen with love.

CONTENTS

1

ORIGINS OF
LIVERPOOL CITY FC

When the Lancashire League held their meeting at the Sandon Hotel in Liverpool on a blisteringly hot day in early June 1893, one of the members of the executive was heard to remark loudly above the throng of chattering voices to their hosts (the board of the newly formed Liverpool Football Club): 'You have the finest team in the league, the finest ground, the finest headquarters and the finest president.' The kind remarks were high praise indeed for the president, John Houlding, and were seen by the executive of the club as a fitting way to begin their victory celebrations as everyone in the room endorsed the sentiments.

For a club that had only just celebrated its first birthday it was also recognition that they were now established. And how could the committee members argue with such a statement, having spent the afternoon playing bowls on the luscious flat green out the back of the bar? And those wanting to stay out of the hot summer's sun had exclusive use of the billiard room to drink, smoke and pot balls to their heart's content. They were also treated to a magnificent spread for their afternoon tea before settling down to the business in hand. The meeting marked not only the end of a rollercoaster ride of a first season for the side who managed to bag three pieces of silverware for the mantelpiece in the saloon bar of the hotel, but also a victory for one of the true pioneers of Merseyside football in Houlding. He oversaw the birth of a team out of the ashes of a bitter internecine dispute at Anfield that almost saw the stadium wave goodbye to football forever only to be saved by football's first mass foreign invasion of players.

The visiting VIPs had descended on his hotel to combine league business with the presentation of the magnificent championship trophy to Houlding and that honour fell to Isaac Smith, the Southport Central president. It was while passing it over he noted how everyone on the board was of the general opinion that the cup had 'come to its rightful resting place,' and the Liverpool board were roundly praised for gaining such success in only their first attempt. It was a great feat indeed, but one that was hard fought and not without a good deal of hard work from those involved.

Everyone gathered demanded a response from Houlding to the kind salutations from the visiting dignitaries by banging their pipes and glasses on the tables. In reply he gave what was on the surface a well earned victory speech at the Sandon, but rather more darkly was a two-fingered salute to those that had tried to destroy him and his newly-formed Liverpool football club in its infancy. The proud Houlding was quick to thank his guests for remembering that although his club was now under a different name, it was still run by many of the same people who had brought league football to the city in the form of Everton. He added that although he had overseen it grow and expand at break-neck speed despite the efforts of some within the city to not only scupper the club, but also to ruin him as a person. Little could he have known or even dreamed that the small acorn he planted with the formation of his beloved team would continue to grow long after his death and would eventually go on to become one of the most successful football clubs this country has ever seen. The location was fitting too as the Sandon Hotel, owned by Houlding, was of particular importance in the history of football on Merseyside. His influence over both the blue and the red sides of the city cannot be understated. He was one of the first people to see the commercial opportunities that football offered and the importance of his role in not only the creation of both Everton and Liverpool, but also their development into the great sides of today, was absolutely crucial.

It is impossible to start any story about Liverpool football team without beginning with their bitter rivals Everton who were at this time the biggest team in the area by quite some margin and reputed to be the richest club in the country. It was not always the case though as there was a period on Merseyside when Bootle, or 'Brutal Bootle' as they were affectionately known by those that played against them, had the bragging rights within the city and were the dominating force within the local football scene. Everton and then Liverpool came later on as the popularity of the sport mushroomed in the Victorian era.

The sport had never been so well supported as it was now, as the popularity of the game snowballed throughout the 19th century. More and more teams

11

were popping up, but before this point the football clubs that did exist were all amateur and pretty much the preserve of very wealthy London gentleman's clubs or public schools such as Eton and Charterhouse—both these teams retained their amateur status and still play to this day. The Barnes club of west London are said to be the oldest football team in the country and date back as far as 1838, although there are no official records of their matches until 1862 when they played local side Richmond and the result was noted. The Sheffield Club (no relation to either Wednesday or United of today) also have a claim to this title because, although they were formed much later in 1857, theirs is a matter of record.

With these new teams came the inevitable governing body as the Victorians were very big on everything being in its place and this was a time of great explorers roaming the planet to shoot, capture and make a record of everything. And so it was that the Football Association (FA) was created in 1863 to oversee the new sport and give it some structure. It was not, however, the great panacea one might have imagined as its creation was rather a shambolic affair.

The governing body was created with the basic idea of agreeing a set of universal rules as many teams, like you might find when you play a game of pool in a different pub, had their own local twist to the game. The sport had taken refuge on the playing fields of the public school system after it was outlawed by successive governments and there it developed so randomly that each of these in turn had their own versions of how to play it. The first general rules were said to have been agreed around

1848 when representatives from the academic powerhouses of Eton, Rugby, Harrow, Winchester and Shrewsbury all got together to thrash out some common laws which went on to become known as the Cambridge Rules in honour of where the meeting took place.

The game was still a distant cousin to what we know today with the ball allowed to be caught and the offside rule was so strict that it pretty much made passing the ball forwards impossible. Despite reaching an agreement the rules were still widely ignored as the individual public schools continued with their own style in the bloody-minded fashion that characterised the Victorian upper-classes and also because the games had developed their own rules so as to fit into the hugely varied spaces provided as playing fields—or in the case of Charterhouse in the long narrow corridor inside the old monastery.

Rugby and Eton still caught the ball, at Rugby you could run with the ball while at Eton a catch earned you a free-kick. At Winchester the game was played on a long, thin pitch and dribbling was in fact banned. They also differed on the amount of actual violence you could dish out to opponents—the spectrum ranged from plenty to gratuitous which bordered on lethal. But their days were to be numbered as the sport was about to get a new lease of life. Public participation in the game had been growing outside these dusty bastions of education as the public fell back in love with the game. A form of football had been seen in this country throughout medieval times and is said to have dated back to hundreds of years before then. The sport developed throughout the middle ages into a particularly vicious game played between teams of random numbers which were virtually whole towns or villages. The game was little more than a police endorsed riot against a neighbouring village in which wide scale thuggery and violence ruled. These games were eventually outlawed and the popularity of the game dipped dramatically. As far as records show there was plenty of broken bones, but only one death. An act of parliament in 1835 that banned football from the Highways looked to be the final nail in the coffin as there was little green space in the new industrial towns emerging all over the country in the machine led Victorian era and so the game retreated to the vast green spaces of the public schools and the more rural areas away from the working classes. The sport was not to die out though and gained support from an unlikely source—the clergy.

Cricket was by far the biggest sport in the country at this time and many football teams were first formed in a bid to keep a local cricket team, most of which were run by the church, active during the closed season. Everton were one of these new breed of working class teams and were formed in 1878 by the Reverend B.S. Chambers of St Domingo's church. But pretty quickly the sport was to be recognised in its own right as it grew in popularity and the team was now attracting players that were not necessarily connected with the parish so they changed their name to reflect the fact they were representing not the church but the Everton district in Liverpool, by now one of the biggest wards in the country with just short of 30,000 people living within it.

No longer welcome within the confines of the church, history has it that the new side first met at the Queen's Head Hotel in Village Street adjacent to 'Ye Anciente Everton Toffee House'. From this first meeting they gained their rather distinctive and original nickname of 'The Toffees'. Britain's sea power was at its height and Liverpool was a vital hub for trade around the planet. Sugar and cotton were the main imports at the time and as a result made the town into one of refiners and sweet makers while the cotton was offloaded to the mill towns across rain soaked Lancashire as the precious cargo was more pliable and easier to work on the looms in the damp conditions of places like Bolton and Blackburn.

As the century went on the game was brought to the masses mainly through the church, which although on a steady decline still evident today, wielded extraordinary power over the population. It was the simplicity of football over cricket that was the real attraction as cricket needed huge amounts equipment such as pads, bats or stumps as well as a large area of grass for cricket. Just a ball and a makeshift goal were enough to get a football match underway and the game could be played on the backstreets of the big towns as well as the countryside. The latter half of this century was one of great social change in this country as the population had to deal with life after the financially crippling Napoleonic wars. Poverty was widespread as was disease, unemployment and drink fuelled crime. Sport, and football in particular, was seen by the church as a healthy distraction for the more unfortunate in society. The clergy felt that it built character as well as social bonds between people through interaction and group play. It was also seen as a good way to avoid the widespread illnesses such as Cholera through exercise and healthy living. The ruling classes at the time bemoaned general state of the poor and were worried that so few were able to be called up in times of war because they were so weak and enfeebled.

And so it was in 1863 that 12 clubs and schools from the London area met in a dimly lit back room of the Freemason's Tavern in Covent Garden under the guidance of the chairman, Ebenezer Cobb Morley of the Barnes club. The purpose was to define the future of this blossoming sport by adapting the widely disregarded Cambridge Rules and set out a new set of 13 laws that would govern and shape the rather unruly sport into the game we know today. These laws favoured the kicking of the ball and wanted an end to the use of hands in the sport. Each of the laws was concise and they could be pinned to the wall of a changing room to remind the players of what was right and what was wrong.

The FA also outlawed the tactic of 'hacking', or the kicking of an opponent's shins, in order to get the ball from them. The Blackheath side of south east London were founder members of the FA, but withdrew from the meeting in protest over the banning of 'hacking' and instead turned their back on association football and became a successful rugby football club which still operates today. It is important to note that none of the public schools were represented at these meetings as they were not being run by any of their 'chaps' and they snubbed the goings-on.

The Football Association Laws of 1863 as published in the press in December 1863 were as follows:

The maximum length of the ground shall be 200 yards (180 m), the maximum breadth shall be 100 yards (91 m), the length and breadth shall be marked off with flags; and the goal shall be defined by two upright posts, eight yards (7 m) apart, without any tape or bar across them.

A toss for goals shall take place, and the game shall be commenced by a place kick from the centre of the ground by the side losing the toss for goals; the other side shall not approach within 10 yards (9.1 m) of the ball until it is kicked off.

After a goal is won, the losing side shall be entitled to kick-off, and the two sides shall change goals after each goal is won.

A goal shall be won when the ball passes between the goal-posts or over the space between the goal-posts (at whatever height), not being thrown, knocked on, or carried.

When the ball is in touch, the first player who touches it shall throw it from the point on the boundary line where it left the ground in a direction at right angles with the boundary line, and the ball shall not be in play until it has touched the ground.

When a player has kicked the ball, any one of the same side who is nearer to the opponent's goal line is out of play, and may not touch the ball himself, nor in any way whatever prevent any other player from doing so, until he is in play; but no player is out of play when the ball is kicked off from behind the goal line.

In case the ball goes behind the goal line, if a player on the side to whom the goal belongs first touches the ball, one of his sides shall be entitled to a free kick from the goal line at the point opposite the place where the ball shall be touched. If a player of the opposite side first touches the ball, one of his sides shall be entitled to a free kick at the goal only from a point 15 yards (14 m) outside the goal line, opposite the place where the ball is touched, the opposing side standing within their goal line until he has had his kick.

If a player makes a fair catch, he shall be entitled to a free kick, providing he claims it by making a mark with his heel at once; and in order to take such kick he may go back as far as he pleases, and no player on the opposite side shall advance beyond his mark until he has kicked.

No player shall run with the ball.

Neither tripping nor hacking shall be allowed, and no player shall use his hands to hold or push his adversary.

A player shall not be allowed to throw the ball or pass it to another with his hands.

No player shall be allowed to take the ball from the ground with his hands under any pretence whatever while it is in play.

No player shall be allowed to wear projecting nails, iron plates, or gutta-percha on the soles or heels of his boots.

The game still had amateur status at this point and because of this it was not well regulated. The matches that took place were all friendly fixtures and tended to be hastily thrown together affairs rather than particularly well organised matches. In fact these were notoriously badly run as they did little to help promote the sport. Kick-off times were rarely as advertised in the local press and sometimes entire games were abandoned because opposition teams would not turn up after being offered a better deal (more money) to play somewhere else at the eleventh hour, much to the disgust of the supporters, and some of the players, who had their time wasted by turning up to the wrong venue. The sport was on the cusp of becoming huge and to many within the game it became clear that a more structured approach was needed if this amazing growth was to continue.

Probably the biggest turning point for the sport came after the Trade Union Act of 1871 as the unions pushed for a change in the working week. While skilled and office workers had the weekend off, the Act ensured the unskilled majority of the workforce of this country were eventually only obligated to work a half day on Saturday which enabled them to have the afternoon off for leisure pursuits. This in turn produced a gap that sport was soon to fill as a popular form of entertainment—none more so than football. The game fitted this bill perfectly with its rough-and-ready combination of aggression and skill and soon huge crowds were drawn to matches as folk wanted to cheer on their local team or participate themselves to let off some steam.

With the swelling of the number of teams and supporters over the next two decades came an increase in money within the game. So much so that players could now be paid a token fee for playing a match. Professionalism was creeping into the sport despite the best efforts of the FA to battle against it. The game was fast changing from the players paying to represent the club to one in which they were given money for their travelling expenses and also to compensate some for the loss of a day's work. Increasingly players were being paid to play for their clubs, but it was done with a nod and a wink rather than an actual pay packet. There were many ways that a decent player could earn a living from the game despite its amateur status through expenses and bonuses. One particular under-the-counter trick would be for a wealthy owner of club to employ a player at their firm in a bid to encourage them to sign for his team and leave a rival one. The player himself would sometimes never actually do a day's work for his new employer, but be on the books nonetheless and gratefully accept the handsome wage that came with the new position.

It was becoming abundantly clear in the take-off years of the sport between 1870 and 1890 that it was being split into two very distinct camps with the dramatic rise of the sport in the industrial heartlands of the Midlands and the northwest. These new clubs wanted to take football down the professional route and with it pay an 'honest' wage to their players. These few were pitted against the public schools of the south that either would not or could not follow them down that particular road.

Teams such as Corinthians refused point blank to give up their amateur ideals and firmly believed that association football, like rugby football, should do the same. The Corinthian spirit has gone down in romantic legend as one of a gentleman amateur who played for the love of the game and it is said they resented the very idea of a penalty kick on the basis that no player would deliberately foul an opponent, certainly not a gentleman anyway. It is said they would kick the ball wide when awarded one themselves! The public schools simply baulked at the idea of paying their pupils to play a recreational game. Professionalism in rugby was still a century away, but in football it was rapidly becoming the biggest issue within the game. The fear of the FA was that with money comes the possibility of corruption as happened in boxing, horse racing and more recently cricket. The fear of the teams was that without payment they would be missing out on the best players as they would not be able to take time off work and the game would remain the preserve of the rich.

In Scotland the view was much the same as the London-based sides with the Scottish Football Association (SFA) trying many different tactics to stop their players moving south where the money was. The SFA was founded some 10 years after their English counterparts on 13 March 1873 at a meeting held at Dewar's Hotel, Glasgow, attended by representatives of eight clubs, Clydesdale, Dumbreck, Glasgow Eastern, Granville, Queen's Park, Rovers, Third Lanark and Vale of Leven. Officials appointed were: President—Mr A. Campbell; Hon treasurer—Mr W. Ker; Hon secretary—Mr A. Rae; Committee— Messrs W.E. Dick, R. Gardner, W. Gibb, E. Hendry, D. McFarlane, J. McIntyre, J. McKay and J. Turnbull.

With no organising body in existence north of the border and football in Scotland comprising mainly of a series of friendly matches, some with English clubs, Queen's Park, Scotland's oldest and best-known club at that time, took the dramatic step of joining the FA in 1870 and they were one of the clubs which entered the initial FA Cup in 1871–72. Along with each of the other entrants they paid the sum of one guinea towards the cost of the trophy. Other Scottish clubs that played in the English Cup, as the competition was known then, were Third Lanark, Cowlairs, Rangers, Renton and Partick Thistle. Following on from the birth of the SFA, Scotland's own knockout cup competition, the Scottish FA Cup was not far behind. It was first competed for in the 1873–74 season, with Queen's Park being the winners.

The metamorphosis of the sport from the grubby amateur sport into the beautiful game of today owes a lot to the eventual acceptance of professionalism. The former was by no means the idyllic game of yesteryear played by gentlemen on the glorious fields of places like Eton immortalised in *Tom Brown's Schooldays*. Far from it, the game was a violent and vicious pastime played by the upper classes that went hand in hand with all the other unspeakable goings on in those boarding schools between unruly the sons of the landed gentry. The FA knew it was swimming against the tide and legalised professionalism on 20 July 1885 in a bid to rid the game of backhanded payments to players. Now, for the first time, players could earn an 'honest' living from the burgeoning game. Everton were quick to embrace these new changes and for the start of the 1885–86 season they signed three talented professional players in George Dobson from Bolton Wanderers, George Farmer from Oswestry and Job Wilding from Wrexham Olympic to vastly improve their side. And while players had always been paid in some form or another, if there was no money at the club then they went without. This was not the case anymore.

The advent of professionalism owed a lot to Billy Sudell, the fiery manager of the Preston North End side that earned the title 'invincibles' as they stormed to the inaugural league title without losing a match as well as picking up the FA Cup to boot to complete the first ever double. The northwest was a footballing festival and Sudell's men were the headline act. A local lad, privately educated in Cheshire, Sudell soon recognised the success of clubs like Darwen and Blackburn, not just in terms of winning games, but also financially. These were making huge amounts of money from the sport and Sudell took it to the next level. His idea was to manufacture a team rather than rely on the best of the local talent and cast his net wide in a bid to assemble a winning side.

Sudell was the Simon Cowell of his day looking for players with the X-factor and pretty much from the start Preston were a money making franchise and were unashamedly the first ever professional team. His process was to make him as many enemies as it did friends as, possibly out of frustration, more likely out of his single minded desire to get his own way, he did not bother with any pretence about the fact that he was paying the best players to come to his club in order to win trophies. Nonetheless, one thing was clear. His policy was a spectacular success. Throughout the early 1880s his handpicked side of players from all over Britain were dishing out the good news to every team they met. In some cases the scores were so unflattering and the games utterly one-sided they were never invited to play again and were howled at by disgusted opposition fans.

The rumblings in Lancashire were becoming more than a little local difficulty for the FA as their protests became louder as more and more clubs wanted to compensate players and their companies for the day's wages of a player who participated on a Saturday in a bid to compete with teams like Preston North End. The FA argued if they were to allow the payment for one day then why not five or six? It would be the end of amateurism within the sport. The FA won the first battle, but not the war as more teams were now importing players from around the country. Eventually they relented on the paying of expenses for matches and introduced rule 15 which stated:

> Any member of the club receiving remuneration or consideration of any sort above his actual expenses, and any wages actually lost by any such player taking part in any match, shall be debarred from taking part in either Cup, Inter-Association, or International contests and any club employing such player shall be excluded from this Association.

It was not a solution to the problem, more of a half-way house as the new guardians of the sport tried to please everyone concerned. As is usual when an issue is fudged, it in fact appealed to no-one as it was neither meat nor fish and the matter came to a head soon after in the winter of 1884. On 19 January Sudell's side played an FA Cup tie against Upton Park in front of a packed Deepdale. A complaint was made regarding the eligibility of some of the players in his side under this rule. The game ended in a 1–1 draw but before Preston could take part in the replay Sudell was hauled in front of the FA to answer the charges and despite his protestations they were thrown out of the competition, but fortunately the FA did not go the whole way and expel them from the Association too. Sudell was furious and he was not alone. While he lost this test case against the FA he won a lot of sympathy from the other Lancashire clubs. He openly admitted he had paid players to join his club from around the country, but that his method of recruiting players did not contravene rule 15. He vowed to get revenge and in October of that year he gathered together a group of rebel clubs that also had simmering resentment to being told what to do and had decided to join forces and make a stand against the FA. If Preston were guilty then so were just about every other team in Lancashire, including some of the biggest clubs of the day, to varying degrees. They met with the intention of forming their own breakaway British Football Association. Their move proved to be an even more popular one than they imagined as a huge number clubs quickly flocked to their banner and left the FA facing the very real threat of the wealthiest and best supported clubs defecting. These were militant times away from the sport with the rise of the trade unions in the work place and in the end the FA called for all concerned to meet in London the following January.

The great showdown between the Football Association and the supporters of professionalism took place in London on 19 January 1885 before the biggest assembly ever mustered in the history of the FA. Such was the interest within the sport that no less than 221 clubs and associations were represented at the historic meeting that was to define the future of the sport in the Freemasons Tavern, where the FA had been founded a generation before.

The FA's Charles Alcock, a former player and at this time on the board at Wanders FC, proposed 'that it is desirable to legislate for professionalism under most stringent conditions'. He was no fan of the idea, but he was a realist and understood that compromise was the only way forward. Not all agreed, indeed there was some dissent. But Sudell by now knew there was a mood for change in the air and, amidst great cheers from his supporters, rose to put forward his claim that professionalism was alive and well, not only in Lancashire, but it was also known in Birmingham and Sheffield. His reasoning was that wherever you had big gates, crowds and their gate receipts you would always get professionalism. It was better to have it out in the open rather than professionals thinly disguised as amateurs. The FA were in effect criminalising people for making a living out of the sport they loved and people were willing to pay to watch. He said:

> Preston are all professionals, but if you refuse to legalize them then they will be amateurs. We shall be amateurs and there is nothing you can do about it.

His arguments were backed up by Harry Chambers, a founder of the original Sheffield club, who said the FA was founded without the Lancashire clubs and if they did not agree to allow them to stop the pretence and pay their player openly and honestly then they could carry on without them.

The, at times, raucous two-and-a-half hour meeting was drawn to a close and votes on the amendment were cast. The voting went for Sudell and Alcock to the tune of 113 against 108, for the motion and so, although they won, the resolution failed to get the necessary two-thirds majority to carry it. Within two months another meeting of the FA, on 23 March 1885, the same proposal was put, this time by Dick Gregson, the secretary of the Lancashire FA, seconded by Preston North End under Sudell and again the motion was defeated, but this time by an even narrower margin of 106 to 69. A third, and ultimately final meeting on this subject was held on 20 July 1885 and the motion was passed as much by the fact that the majority of clubs chose to use their veto by not turning up rather than voting for the idea so it could be argued that Sudell had not so much won as the opposition had surrendered. Nonetheless, the outcome was clear—English football had gone professional.

While everyone was getting used to the new rules and pushing the boundaries it was only a matter of time before someone fell foul of the change in circumstances. And it was Everton. The club were banned for a month from the Liverpool and District Football Association after being found to have used players who were not signed on at the club in 1888. In short they were accused of fielding ringers in order to win a local cup tournament. The players, all Scottish, were named as Cassidy, Goudie, Dick, Watson, Weir, Izatt and Murray. As punishment the secretary of the association visited the team's new headquarters in the Sandon Hotel to remove the L&D Association Cup they had just won for the third time and the Everton board put a tiny headstone in its place to mourn the loss.

The game as a whole was crying out for a visionary to take it forward to secure its future and found one in the chairman of Aston Villa, William McGregor. The Scotsman came up with the brilliant idea of a league system in which teams would guarantee to play each other on set days. This was to stamp out the haphazard nature of the friendlies and allow the teams to promote their game through the press and with a set schedule the fans would also know which grounds to be at on particular days to cheer their team on.

The wise McGregor had the foresight to see that if the game was to have any future then it lay in a professional approach to the whole affair and could not carry on in its amateur manner as they now had wages bills to meet. McGregor invited representatives from a select band of five teams to join him at Anderton's Hotel in London to thrash out a league format on 23 March 1888. These were Blackburn Rovers, Bolton Wanderers, Preston North End, West Bromwich Albion and Aston Villa. An open application was given to the other clubs in the country and the founding five then had to choose a further seven to join them in the first league from all the teams that applied. The idea was to have six wholly professional clubs from the Midlands and another half a dozen professional teams from the northwest. Joining the famous five would be Wolverhampton Wanderers, Notts County, Stoke, Burnley, Accrington Stanley, Derby County and Everton. These fortunate few were invited to a second meeting at the Royal Hotel in Manchester on 17 April 1888 where the rules of participation within the league were drawn up. The inclusion of the last team was a contentious one at the time because the biggest team in the Merseyside region was in fact Bootle, but the clincher was the fact that Everton had a purpose built stadium in Anfield that was able to accommodate a large, fee paying group of supporters and therefore provide the necessary financial basis for a professional side.

The Perthshire born McGregor was a tremendous football fan and held every honorary office at Aston Villa in his time. He was desperate to promote the sport that he so loved to the wider public and enable it to grow. To do this he knew he would have to devise a way in which the best players remained in the game and this would mean paying them a steady salary. Wages, though, would be wholly dependent on good attendances and so he came up with a plan in which the top 12 teams in the country would agree to play each other on a regular basis and put an end to the shambolic practice of friendly matches. This was the start of the professional league system that is in place today. The league quickly raised the standard of football as a whole within the country and as such the players became commodities for hire and to trade. The better players would attract bigger crowds and therefore more money for their clubs. The stars of the day were paid more money to reflect this newfound status, a model that is still in operation today. Albeit with one major difference, the FA wanted to cap the wages in order to stop the wealthier clubs pooling the best talent by virtue of having a bigger bank balance. By the end of the 1891–92 season Everton had a dozen players on their books earning £3 a week—this was around double the average working wage of the day. But the club had the crowds to match and were getting gates of close to 14,000 people while their still amateur neighbours Bootle could only attract a third of that at best.

Many other clubs applied to join the league, but numbers were limited to a dozen because McGregor and the other committee members realised they could only guarantee 22 dates throughout the first season as many shared their grounds with, or rather were the winter guests of, cricket teams who played throughout the summer. Each founding member was to agree to a number of rules including to play their strongest available team in every match under a penalty of forfeiting their position in the league if they did not. These were of course days long before wealthy clubs could look down on certain cup competitions and deplorably play their second string or, in the case of some, their youth sides in a bid to coast through to the next round without risking injury to some of the higher paid employees.

With payments to players now legal in England and professional footballers being paid decent salaries for that time, many Scottish players headed southwards to ply their trade, whereas in Scotland the game remained, in theory anyway, an amateur game until 1893. In a bid to stop their players being tempted by what was happening over the border the Scottish Football Association ordered all of its member clubs to withdraw from the English FA and cease further participation in the FA Cup 1887.

The success of the league set-up in England was viewed with some envy by Scotland's top clubs and the drive to set up a rival league in Scotland grew stronger amongst almost all in the Scottish game. The main opposition came from those who worried that the establishment of a league in Scotland would inevitably lead to professionalism coming to Scottish football and Queen's Park Football Club felt so strongly about this that they wanted no part to play in the establishment of the Scottish League and indeed they boycotted the inaugural league season in 1890–91. QPFC's motto was 'Ludere Causa Ludendi' (The Game for the Game's Sake). This sentiment was entirely fitting for an amateur club in an amateur era.

Everton were the poor relations in the newly-formed league system, but their participation was deemed essential by McGregor as they were growing at such a rapid rate as football took hold in Liverpool. They benefitted greatly from the pooling of gate receipts by all the clubs within the league in those early days to ensure wealth was evenly distributed between league members. The club started well with a 2–1 win over Accrington in their league debut at Anfield and they went on to finish in eighth place in the inaugural season having lost only three of their 11 games at home.

In their second year they did far better than anyone could have foreseen and were even tied at the top with the defending champions, Preston's famous 'Invincibles,' with a game to go but were unable to find one last win and the title remained at Deepdale. It was a case of third time lucky for Everton as they grew from founding members to being crowned champions within three years as Fred Geary stamped his name on the records books as the club's first ever goal scoring hero—netting 20 times in 22 matches, including 11 in the opening six games.

But good times on the pitch only papered over the cracks that were beginning to show at board level and kept the more mutinous members in line. Everton won their first league title in 1891 and had just built an impressive new stand to cope with their larger than ever crowds. What was to follow was an incredibly dark and shameful chapter in Everton's history. A schism that shook the club to its very core and forced the board, players and fans to choose between two warring factions within the club and culminated in the birth of Liverpool Football Club.

2

THE SPLIT

It was soon after the Everton side were crowned the kings of English football that the wheels came off of their celebrations in quite spectacular fashion. Some particularly vicious infighting that had been simmering below the surface boiled over and would result in the club coming close to folding. The ill-feeling that had grown from petty grievances and jealousies was to spread like a cancer through the corridors of power before exploding into a full-blown power struggle at the heart of the club—and it was to come to a head throughout the next season and split the club right down the middle.

The result was that the board was divided into two quite distinct camps that could not be reconciled. On one side was the Dublin-educated George Mahon who went on to become a senior partner in a prominent local accountant firm Roose, Mahon & Howard and a founding member of the club. The privately educated Mahon represented the establishment. On the other was the club president and owner of Anfield, John Houlding, a self-made business man and entrepreneur with a 'can-do' attitude. Stuck in the middle was John McKenna who was the friend of the players and staff at the club. Mahon was born in Liverpool, but spent his childhood in Ireland after his family moved there in his infancy only to return in adulthood.

Their dispute was a historic one as the 39-year-old Mahon was a long time opponent of Houlding and their mutual loathing was based in politics, rather than sport, as the pair had clashed previously over the ballot box. Around this time the political landscape in Liverpool was completely different to that of today as the city was ruled by the Conservative party. Life on the streets was tough as it was plagued by an increase in crime fuelled by a wide-scale drink problem that was mirrored throughout Britain at the time.

The excessive drinking of alcohol had long been tolerated and even promoted during the early part of the 19th century. With diseases running rife throughout the major cities because of poor sanitation and a lack of clean drinking water, the drinking of alcoholic beverages was seen by many as a healthy alternative to what was available. It would be naïve to say that no one died through drinking gin, but it would be difficult to prove that anyone got Typhoid or Smallpox through downing a measure of 'mother's ruin'. This country's relationship with alcohol has been a long and difficult one. The Gin Act of 1736 sought to stamp out the lawlessness and social deprivation linked with the spirit by simply banning the consumption of it. Riots followed and the government of the day had to back down over the ban. The publication of William Hogarth's *Gin Lane* in 1751 gave a graphic description of the havoc that drink was wreaking among the less fortunate in society and in particular the poor of inner-city London.

By 1830 the Beer Act was passed to curb the abuse of spirits. The thinking of the day was that people turned to gin because the beer was of such a low quality down to the lack of free trade within the business. With so few brewers, the Act made it possible for anyone to buy a license to brew and sell beer in their own home for a cost of just two guineas. Within a few months around 25,000 of these licenses were granted and this resulted in an explosion in competition and as a result the consumption of alcohol went through the roof.

Just like the introduction of the 24-hour drinking rule in recent years in the misguided hope of curbing drinking by increasing the public's access to it only increased the amount of alcohol related admissions to hospital. The drinking culture in this country was transformed in the Victorian era, but not in a positive way. The country was becoming industrialised at an alarming rate and the last thing that employers wanted or needed was a drunken workforce operating the new and highly dangerous machinery. As a result the Temperance movement developed from the 1830s and by 1853 was organised into a quite formidable political pressure group called the UK Alliance. It argued for teetotalism, and for the right of ratepayers to ban the drinks trade in their own town.

The movement was being driven by the church and the Liberal party that held a strong anti-drinking stance and linked the trouble in society with alcohol, via the brewing industry in the city, and pointed the finger squarely at the Conservatives, whose party was swelled by a number of prominent people in the drinks trade. This was a peak in the support of the movement and led to the Liberals making massive in-roads into the core Tory vote—Mahon was one of this new breed of tea-total Liberals while Houlding was a long standing Conservative and local purveyor of alcoholic drinks. This set the two at loggerheads from the start and was the reason behind their mutual distrust.

From humble beginnings, Houlding went on to become a wealthy man through the ever-expanding drinks industry and was the producer of 'Houlding Sparkling Ales'. He was one of the main beneficiaries of the recent changes in legislation by the government and became immensely wealthy in a short period of time. Born in Tenterden Street, just off Scotland Road in Liverpool, his father ran a small dairy and delivered milk for a living. The business was later to falter due to cattle plague, despite Houlding Junior leaving his job as an office boy at a firm of local shipbuilders, Miners and Rae, to help out with his father's struggling business. He then took a back-breaking job as a porter at the Cotton Exchange before following his father into the drinks trade by working at a local brewery.

Starting off as a general labourer and then becoming a drayman, the young Houlding impressed his bosses with his sheer hard work and endeavour. At the age of just 20, and with no real previous experience to speak of, he was promoted to the lofty post of chief brewer. By 1870, around the same time that the Temperance movement was at its peak, he had saved enough money to build his own brewery in Tynemouth Street which he ran with the help of just one other person and turned out to be a brilliant success. In January 1888 Houlding registered an ancient fire beacon, which stood on the site of St George's church and was known as the Everton Beacon, as the symbol of his brewery to represent his affiliation to the local area. This symbol was also later incorporated into the badge of the Everton football club. While establishing his business from scratch he also found time to keep up his involvement in the local football club. He was now at the height of his powers as a local business man. He also goes down in history as the man who saved Everton's bacon by bringing them to Anfield after they were asked to leave their pitch on Priory Lane.

The place that the club had called home was little more than a piece of scrap wasteland that was converted into a pitch for them to play on and proved adequate in the early days. As the interest grew in the club they introduced ropes around the pitch to stop the ever-increasing number of fans from encroaching on the pitch. The reasons for their eviction from the Priory Lane pitch were unclear to many fans. Some reports suggest it was because the noise from the growing crowds was said to be a menace by the locals, while others say they had difficulty in getting permission to build any changing rooms.

In truth it was no secret that the club were substantially behind with their rent and it is more likely that were thrown off for not paying their bills by their landlord. The club were in trouble and it was left to Houlding to rescue the club from being wound up by flexing his now considerable financial muscle and paying off their debts. The club could not charge the fans to come and see them play as it was impossible to police the crowds and tell those who had paid from those that had not. This severely reduced their chances of making money to balance the books and pay for their expenses. The then Everton board approached Houlding and asked for his help in saving the club from complete and utter collapse by purchasing some land for them to play on and renting it back to the club.

As a result, in September 1884, Houlding bought a

site on Anfield Road that could be used as a pitch from a local man called Joseph Orrell. He made it clear that if the adjoining land across the road belonging to his son John, whom Houlding knew as a fellow brewer and property tycoon, was to be developed in the coming years then there could be a problem as although the pitch was wide enough, the addition of a stand would encroach onto his property.

As it was just an access road at the time, despite Orrell's assertion that he would develop the land at some point, the committee agreed to the clause being inserted into the contract. It proved to be a small but pivotal detail in the birth of Liverpool Football Club in the future, but one that the board readily agreed to. Houlding jumped at the chance to fund the deal and help out the team he supported and immediately handed over almost £6,000 of his own personal fortune in an unsecured loan. Houlding dug deep and had nothing but a hand-written receipt and a shake of the hand as guarantee he would ever get his money back and the club were able to buy the land. Not only that, but they could improve the facilities with a view to charging fans to watch them play games.

This loan would have been the equivalent of £350,000 currently, although land prices in the city have gone up significantly more since the end of the 20th century. Some would say it was an act of great kindness while others would think it one of staggering stupidity not have a contract with the club. It is unlikely such a proposal would have passed the test on *Dragons Den*.

But one thing is certain and that is it proved to be one of magnificent vision by Houlding as it would become an excellent bargaining chip when it came to which clubs were to be permitted to join the first ever league which, although still only being talked about at this point, was close to coming to fruition. Everton could not have afforded to buy the land outright themselves, indeed the local press reported their fundraising attempt only managed to collect a pathetic £11 in total, but Houlding was happy to fork out his hard earned thousands to help the club if they were happy to pay him a peppercorn rent of 4 percent of the loan in return. He was adamant that they should only pay him back when the club were in a position to be able to. In fact, during the first year he happily accepted substantially less than the 4 percent he requested as the club was still finding its feet on strict condition that the club played a benefit match annually to aid the Stanley Hospital in February of each year.

A year later he handed over more money to further upgrade the facilities within the ground which was absolutely necessary if they were to cope with the rapidly increasing numbers of supporters who were turning up to follow their side. The loan paid for a new stand to house the now paying public in relative comfort and also to erect hoardings around the ground to keep out people who had not paid for the pleasure of watching Everton play. Anfield was rapidly becoming one of the finest football grounds in the country thanks mainly to the benevolence of Houlding.

In a speech to the board at the time Houlding said:

I have bought the land and undertaken a great responsibility on your behalf. I am not sure even now that I have acted wisely, but I rely on your honour to see that I get a fair return on my outlay. I understand that at present you can see your way to pay only £100 per annum rental and I am willing to accept this or any less sum warranted by your balance sheets; but if your funds permit, I shall expect at least 4 percent on my outlay. Pay me what you can, and if you cannot pay anything, you need not be afraid of being turned out. As long as I live I intend that the ground is used for football.

The Everton board at the time were delighted with his actions and put forward a special vote of thanks to publicly recognise his breathtaking generosity and welcomed him into the boardroom with open arms. It was not to be the last time he was to dig deep for the club as records show he was to lend the club £180 in 1886–87, £350 in 1887–88, £1,200 in 1888–89 and £600 in 1889–90, although despite these sums being loans he was to see little of it back. The minutes showed that in the same years he received £100 in rent for the first three years, which rose to £200 in 1888–89 and again to £240 in 1889–90, still some way short of the money he was putting into the club every year.

Away from sport, Houlding was rapidly becoming a big noise within the city in his own right and was soon known locally as 'King John of Everton', such was the high regard he was held in. As well as a high profile politician, Houlding was a philanthropist and generous benefactor to many causes within the city. He never forgot his hard upbringing and even though he now was a wealthy man he knew what it meant to be poor. His acts of charity and benevolence within the local community are well documented throughout history and he went on to become a Tory councillor in Everton, easily the most popular ward in the city, in a bid to better serve and improve the lives of his less well-off neighbours. He was a tireless fighter for the poor through the West Derby Union which provided them with health care and workhouses in the absence of any form of the welfare state that we all take for granted now. Houlding, though, was a canny businessman first and foremost and his work within the Union helped him politically as did his involvement in the club which was to prove to be both the making and the breaking of Everton football club. While it is true to say that his loans certainly saved it in its infancy, there was growing resentment from many within that he was exerting too much control over the board. Moreover, he was personally making huge sums of money from the football club as well as using it for political gain as his association with the team helped him on polling day.

Houlding owned many other properties in the city besides Anfield, including the Sandon Hotel close to the ground on a street which bore his name and was just a stone's throw from the ground. This was the place where the board of Everton FC would hold their committee meetings and became a building synonymous with the football club. This is commemorated to this day by a small plaque which has been mounted on the wall. The team also used the bowling pavilion attached to the back of the pub as changing facilities on match days, much to the disgust of some fans who thought it demeaning for a side of the stature of Everton, who had recently won the league, still had to push their way through hordes of fans on a match day in their kit. The team photographs of the day feature the pavilion in the background as they were taken on its steps.

The hotel was to prove a bone of contention among his critics who tried to use it as a stick to beat him with. Houlding provided these premises to the club free of charge when they approached him for help in the early days as an act of kindness. Not only was he paying the gas bill to heat the hot water for the players to use after the match he also kept a back room free for the committee to use during their regular meetings at no cost. His critics though, now growing in confidence and number, claimed his involvement was merely to help with the promotion of his brewery to the committee, the players and a captive match day audience and that these commercial opportunities were his motive rather than goodwill.

These detractors, led by Mahon, said he decreed only products he brewed were allowed to be sold inside the ground to the ever bigger crowds as the team became more successful and he would also benefit from these fans frequenting his pubs outside the stadium before and after the game. That, linked with the interest on his loans, started a whispering campaign at board level that he personally profited greatly from the club and led some to suggest he was making decisions at the club for his own ends. There were in fact no official applications of any sort made to get a license to sell alcoholic drinks of his or anyone else's at the ground during this time and it proved to be one of many untruths spread about Houlding in a cruel and malicious bid to tarnish his reputation within both the club and the city.

If Mahon and his cronies were so bothered then why did they continue to use his rooms free of charge? If meeting in a hotel so offended their morals then what was stopping them moving their committee meetings elsewhere? The battle was being played out in the newspapers of the day as committee members on both sides of the divide sent open letters to the editors demanding answers to many questions such as these and many others to do with the Goodison Road site, the financial situation of Everton and why Mr Mahon had been in touch with other local brewers with regard to financing the move if he was so opposed to alcohol production and consumption. What may also have been behind the scurrilous rumours doing the rounds was the fact that there was a general election due in 1892 so Mahon and others from the Liberal party within the local area may have had more sinister motives for smearing the man.

It is true to say that to this day many Everton fans still believe Houlding was a bad person and one almost destroyed the club through greed. Indeed he has unfairly gone down in the folklore of the club as a pantomime villain to be booed and hissed at whenever his name is mentioned despite being acknowledged only quite recently by the club as one of the six founding fathers of Merseyside football in a nod to the debt the club owes him for their very existence. A portrait of Houlding was commissioned in 2009 and unveiled later that year in the boardroom at Goodison Park alongside another five significant figures within the history of the club in Ben Swift Chambers, John McKenna, George Mahon, James Baxter and Will Cuff. Without all these figures, it is almost certain the club would not exist today. Indeed, on his death in 1902 the Everton players wore black arm bands during their next match out of respect for his passing.

Off the pitch the whole matter of alcohol was becoming a grave national problem and was dominating Westminster debates. The general public's disapproval, or at least the disapproval of the privileged few that had the right to vote, swept William Gladstone's Liberal party into government in the 1868 general election. They, in turn, passed the licensing act of 1872 which resulted in more rioting in the streets and a war of words between the opposing sides of the debate within the House of Commons. As the unrest escalated into fighting on the streets and bordered on revolution, the Liverpool -born Prime Minister realised he could not ban drinking and stay elected and so he brought down the duty on French wine in a bid to introduce a European style drinking culture, but instead was booted out of office and people raised a glass of some of Bordeaux's finest export to toast his removal instead of gin.

As the crime rate in the troubled city of Liverpool was disproportionately higher than the national average it added some weight to the finger pointing from the local Liberals as the political shenanigans carried on. Anecdotal stories of vote rigging as well as various other political stitch-ups are hard to prove, but the rumours persisted about all concerned over the years and were too numerous to simply dismiss out of hand. Both Houlding and Mahon continued to cross swords many times over the years and it soon made them uncomfortable bedfellows on the board of Everton as the distrust and ill-feeling between them grew. And now the two political heavyweights were to slug it out for outright control of the football club as the matter came to a head over a disputed land deal.

The final straw for Houlding's dissenters came when John Orrell, perhaps smelling a business opportunity, threw a spanner in the works by announcing he wanted to exercise his right (agreed to in the initial land deal) to build up the Anfield Road. The city was growing on a daily basis as workers flooded in to fill the dockyards and living space was becoming an issue. His plan would have meant taking down a brand-spanking-new stand the club had just paid a lot of money to have built, but encroached on his land by a few feet, so that he could then erect houses for the expanding numbers of economic migrants arriving in the city to fuel the industrial boom. The loss of the stand would almost certainly have dealt the club a punishing, and probably fatal, financial body-blow and would have thrown the future of football at Anfield in doubt.

Orrell had been in discussion with the club about the stretch of land (just 56 yards wide) on a couple of occasions previously and discussed his intentions to make use of it but it never went further than talk. Now he decided to make good on his investment one way or another and not surprisingly he offered to back down on his plans if the club would concede to pay him a generous rent in return for use of the land next door to the stadium. He wanted to pocket around £120 per annum for the privilege. This was not beyond Everton as the club posted a healthy return of £1,700 that year so while the coffers were not exactly overflowing, they were certainly bulging thanks to the year's successful league campaign.

The problem for many within the hierarchy was that club was already renting the pitch from Houlding, and had done for the previous six years without complaint. The deal he struck with the Everton board meant the rent would gradually rise year-on-year from an original annual fee of £100, which would have been equivalent to just under £5,000 nowadays, as the team became more successful and the crowd attendances rose. It seemed a simple enough agreement struck between gentlemen at the time. When the internal row erupted Everton were, for the first time, paying £250 a year in rent, which amounted roughly to the 4 percent he wanted when he originally agreed to buy the land on behalf of the club. But it would mean the members of the board would be asked to stump up £370 per annum in combined rent to the two men, more than £22,000 currently, for the right to play at Anfield and to train next door on his business associate's land. This was seen by some within the club as a scam that the two brewers had concocted to extort money from the club as Houlding looked to squeeze the club dry and was too bitter a pill for the board to swallow.

In light of the situation the club now found itself, with Orrell's plans to develop the land, Houlding proposed a new deal. Orrell already stated that he would be happy to rent the club the land, but Houlding put a proposal to the board that they all chip in to buy out Orrell and develop the whole stadium complex to use the land as a training ground and build a set of changing rooms there. This did not go down so well with the committee either, which was no surprise bearing in mind the climate of mistrust that was steadily building within the boardroom. The ever forward thinking Houlding decided on a yet another way around the impasse that he felt would satisfy everyone concerned. He proposed a share option to raise the funds needed to buy Anfield from him, and therefore relinquishing his role as landlord to the club, as well as collecting enough cash to secure the adjacent land for the sole use of the players. He wanted to set up a limited liability company to oversee the purchase and the senior committee at the club approved it. His thinking was that it would provide security for the club and leave open the option of expanding the stadium at a later date and enable the building of training facilities of their own and not have to use his hotel. It would instantly render the claims of him trying to milk the club as invalid as he would now no longer be the landlord. Again he was thwarted by Mr Mahon and his cronies as the proposal was defeated when put to the vote of all the members.

They dismissed this as yet another get rich scheme by Houlding despite the assertions from some that the poor performances on the pitch were a direct result of the players' association with the Sandon Hotel. Now it was his fault that the team were playing badly as their defence of the title fell apart. Houlding had already gone to the trouble of putting together plans for a new changing facility for which he commissioned a local firm of reputable architects to design to illustrate his idea, only for the majority of the board to reject them outright. Land prices were low at this time around the country and some within the Everton committee thought the prices he proposed were over inflated and he was trying to offload a failing asset.

There was an element of truth in this as Houlding would have stood to have gained from the land deal, but he was a business man and a successful one at that and he did not gain that mantle by being a soft touch when it came to making deals. It seemed that whatever ideas he came up with or actions he proposed to avoid confrontation, his detractors were hell bent on putting up obstacles at every turn. They even put forward the quite scandalous proposal that Houlding, and not the club, should pay this increase in rent or buy the adjacent land and offer it as a gift to the club. During their negotiations with Orrell he suggested a way out for the club. He requested the club pay him a one-off fee of £100 and in return he would shelve his renovation plans for a year.

The board put this suggestion to the much maligned Houlding, or rather they presented him with a bill for the full amount which, after some consideration and initial willing, he refused to pay and, with Orrell giving the club notice that they had to take down the stands through his solicitors, called for a Special General Meeting of the board on 12 October to settle game of brinkmanship once and for all. His view was that he was now being taken for a ride and if the other members of the board were willing to put their hands in their own pockets he would contribute £20 towards the bill. They were not and now the situation became a Mexican stand-off as these two heavyweights faced each other down with neither wanting to be the one to blink first.

The first salvo was fired by Mahon when he proposed a motion demanding that Houlding quit the club and his role as president and come to an agreement over the tenancy of a reduced rent of £190 for the next five years and an option to extend it to 10. Not to be outdone, Houlding countered with a bombshell of his own by telling the club they had to quit his land. It read:

> Mr John Orrell has given me notice that he intends to exercise his right to make the road on the North side of the Football Field one half viz 18 feet of the breadth of which must be contributed out of my land and one half out of his.
>
> The enclosure & Stands which have been erected on sufferance by private subscription extend over the 18 feet to be contributed by me and I am required by Mr Orrell to remove them forthwith.
>
> Under these circumstances it is with extreme regret that I am compelled to give you notice which I hereby do that you must give up possession of the piece of

land situated between Anfield Road and Walton Breck Road used as a Football Ground with the approaches thereto after the close of the present Season viz. April 30th 1892. This is the date of commencement of your occupation; but if it should appear that there is any doubt about this, you will understand that this notice applies to the expiration of the current year of your occupation whenever it may be.

P.S. As according to rule all finance & property of the Club is vested absolutely in the Committee, I will take an early opportunity of meeting to members to arrange about Stands & other property on the ground.

The bitter power struggle soon spilled out of the boardroom and was fought in the full glare of the fans as offer and counter offer was made but with no agreement in sight. Houlding was slowly being forced out of the club and the board members knew they soon would have to choose sides one by one. The skirmishes now took place during various public meetings in which the rebels discussed the proposed deal by Houlding before negotiating directly with Orrell himself as they tried to secure a long term loan of the land without the help of the brewer. The club proposed to buy the land at the north end of the ground from him at the same price that Houlding had paid almost seven years previously, but Orrell knew he was in a position of strength and refused to drop his prices leaving the board no chance of outflanking Houlding.

As the row dragged on the board were eventually presented with an ultimatum. Either they could keep the status quo and side with Houlding and Orrell which would mean they could stay at Anfield and pay an increased rent in order to do so or leave for a site proposed by Mahon on Mere Green, Goodison Road for a fraction of the rent. The new rent would be roughly £50 per year although they would have to find the funds to build another stadium from scratch over the summer as the site was still a field at this point with none of the facilities they had carefully built over the recent years at Anfield. The battle lines were finally drawn between the two warring factions within the club and it was down to the hierarchy within the club to choose which horse to back.

The arguments raged throughout the autumn and winter months of 1891 and through to the spring of 1892. In January the fans were protesting within the ground with regard to the state of affairs both on and off the pitch. The boardroom bedlam was destabilising the entire club and was blamed by many fans for the poor performances on the pitch as the club put up a pathetic defence of their title as it slipped further and further into crisis. A letter to the editor of *Field Sports* in mid-February summed up the feelings of the fans at the time and still has echoes today for anyone who has watched their once proud club crumble from the top down. 'As an old player and member who has taken little or no part in ground dispute' went the letter which the writer cryptically signed himself off as 'C':

> I trust you will grant me a little space to warn the members against the seductive influence of debating society oratory to which they have been treated to at the general meetings of the club . . . every member of the club as well as its supporters, putting aside all the ground disputes etc, must be weary and sick of the repeated defeats which the club has sustained week after week.
>
> It is palpable that there is a screw loose somewhere. To my mind it can only be put down to mismanagement and want of organising ability on

the part of the executive, and as it has been a proud boast on the part of one section of the committee that they are in a majority then it is clear that all affairs of the club connected with games—viz, engaging of players, selecting of teams etc—must practically have been carried out by them. In short the disastrous results of the season have occurred when this said section have 'held the reins'.

. . . In conclusion, I would state that had the committee managed things in a more business like way the question of the ground would never have assumed such a serious aspect, and in fairness to the members who elected them to their positions, they ought now to retire en bloc, and leave the question of their re-election with the new members, when, I fancy there would be a few changes that would be of advantage of the club.

The advent of professionalism within football turned a sporting pastime into a business and, as such, a money making vehicle for owners and chairmen alike. Houlding, though, had been seen by a growing cabal of board members within the club as making too much personal profit. The in-fighting was taking its toll on Houlding personally as he was by now fast approaching his sixtieth birthday and of failing health. Tempers were becoming short and during one of their exchanges he is said to have given the club notice to quit as he wanted an end to the matter. For 'C' and everyone else at the club the end of the stand-off was close as it was clear the argument and counter-arguments had pushed the situation beyond 'the point of no return'.

Mahon and his followers who were now running the club in all but name as supporters of Houlding were removed from positions of power one by one. A short meeting towards the end of January resulted in them coming back to Houlding asking him to consider accepting a lesser rent of around £180 per annum as well as signing a contract that handed the ownership of all the stands to the club and not the landlord and gave him just days to agree. It was now a matter of principle and both Houlding and McKenna were not men to be brow beaten or bullied into anything and so they refused to agree to this. The deadline was then extended to seven days 'to give them more time to think about the deal' before another committee meeting extended the deadline again by a further week. A special meeting was called on a wet night on 3 March 1892 when Everton took official steps to part company with Houlding. He was now no longer able to sign cheques for the club or nominate people on the board.

The final gathering was little more than a kangaroo court on Tuesday 15 March with the club president on trial. Amid utterly disgraceful scenes that would have shamed a Labour party conference in the mid-eighties, Houlding's reputation was attacked and when he, or other original members of the board like McKenna, tried to recall how he saved the club from being wound up not long before they were heckled and shouted down by members with short memories, indeed Houlding was even called 'a Shylock' by one.

Despite their best efforts to put his side of the argument to the members present at the fateful witch hunt of a meeting to strip him of his presidency and expel him from the club only 18 of the 500 that attended and voted were on his side. A more one-sided a debate could not have been contrived by Mahon and his band of rebels. This majority was made up of the new breed of board members who had joined recently and had no memory of how Houlding had helped the club in its infancy and were taken in by the whispering campaign. But the deed had been done and now there was no way back. The whole sorry affair had reached its sad conclusion and the exodus of top brass, players, coaching staff and fans to Goodison Road began at the end of the season and Houlding was unjustly cast into history as a bad person to be forever despised by all connected with Everton football club. Their last game at Anfield ended in a 3–3 draw with Burton Swifts. The home side came back from 3–1 down to earn a draw with crowd favourite Fred Geary hitting a late equaliser.

The players were not exempt from the turmoil at the top with the free-scoring Geary, now a hero amongst the fans, being used as a pawn in the powerbrokers' game as the following extract from *Field Sports* in June 1892 highlights.

> The difficulties between the Everton club and their players still continue. The latest trouble is with Fred Geary, who was brought before the committee the other evening and requested to give up the management of the public house that he now holds on the grounds that such an occupation was prejudicial to his future play. Geary point blank refused to do anything of the kind. He stated that when he signed an undertaking was come to that he should have a position in Mr Houlding's employ. For some time he served in a junior capacity, and when a vacancy occurred he was given the management of his present house, and on the strength of the promises made he had got married and was very comfortable. He also pointed out that his football agreement was that he should keep himself fit and well to play football, and until he broke the agreement he denied the right of the committee to interfere with his private arrangements. The committee finding Geary unmoveable asked if he would take employ in

another public house. This Geary also refused. He said that since he had been in Mr Houlding's employ he had found everything satisfactory. Mr Houlding had been very kind to him and under the circumstances he had no intention to change. He added that if the committee were agreeable he was quite prepared to sever his links with the club, take his papers back and put an end to the present trouble.

In the face of his threat to walk out on the club if they tried to take away his livelihood it was no surprise that the committee backed down and Geary, one of the top earners at the club, went on to become the first ever goal scorer at Goodison Park. He is fondly remembered as the first of a long line of excellent strikers at the club thanks to his return of 86 goals in 98 appearances. He marked his England debut against Ireland in 1890 with a well taken hat-trick. He did however return to Anfield as a player a few years later. Stricken by injuries towards the end of his career, he signed for Liverpool in 1895 for a fee of £60 where he bagged 14 goals in 45 appearances before returning to Everton where he worked as a groundsman.

The remaining Everton members took just a matter of months to turn the wasteland that was the Mere Green Field into Goodison Park which was officially opened on 24 August 1892. Press reports of the time estimated 12,000 spectators turned up on that balmy Wednesday evening to watch the team compete in a number of amusing sporting events such as the 120 yard dash, high jump and a three-legged race. They ended the spectacle with a firework display. Around 10,000 turned up for the friendly match against Bolton Wanderers that preceded the first league match on 3 September against Nottingham Forest—ending in a 2–2 draw.

The decision of the rebels must have hurt Houlding on a personal level because no matter what the reasons for their dispute, it cannot be denied that he stopped the club from being dissolved only a few years earlier by securing them a pitch to play on at Anfield. He personally sunk thousands of pounds of his own money to buy a piece of land he did not even want and handed it over to a club on the strength of a few promises which were ruthlessly broken. The dispute hit him hard in the heart as well as the wallet as his health deteriorated significantly during the whole débâcle.

How quickly the dream of bringing the magnificent game of football to the working man in Liverpool had turned sour for Houlding. All the early goodwill had been forgotten and friendships ruined by the actions of a few Johnny-come-latelies who had invested a fraction of the money that Houlding had in the club. None of this was to matter as the deed was done although he did, however, find himself in the rather odd position of having a first rate stadium but no team to play in it.

This situation would not last for long as the irrepressible Houlding was a man of action and within days called a meeting in the Neptune Hotel in Clayton Square to publicly announce the creation of a rival to Everton FC with others who had left the club with him. He had been holding meetings with the associates who stayed loyal to him following the acrimonious split in his house on Anfield Road to discuss the forming of a team. Houlding will have taken great comfort from the fact that the majority of these were the same that had built Everton in the early days. These were the 'old guard' that remembered how far the club had come in a short time with Houlding's backing and now they were to go through the same process again.

Amusingly, he wanted to keep the name of Everton by registering 'Everton Football Club and Athletic Grounds Company, Limited' with Companies House in London. This idea was quickly rejected by the FA as they did not want two clubs called Everton battling it out and would only allow one club bearing that name to compete in the league—the one that bore it already. It was time to think big for Houlding if he was going to put together a new team like a phoenix from the ashes of the split. He did just that and went for the name of Liverpool Football Club to reflect that this new side was to be a club for everyone in the city as a whole rather than just those in the local borough of Everton. And so a club that would go on to become one of the most successful teams in the history of the sport was born. He quickly installed himself as president with Edwin Berry as chairman, William E. Barclay as secretary, a role he held at the former club and, crucially, John McKenna was chosen to oversee the team affairs with Barclay to help. The appointment of McKenna was to prove the key to the future success of the club.

McKenna's involvement in Liverpool was arguably the making of the fledgling club. He proved to be one of the most interesting characters to have ever been involved in the beautiful game and was instrumental shaping the new team. When he died, his obituary in the *Telegraph* of Monday 23 March 1936 called him 'one of the most remarkable characters in Association Football'. That is quite a testament written in a time long before the screaming tabloid headlines of today. It is right that his many deeds in the game should be dusted down and revisited and that this man is remembered in football because his achievements within the game are many.

McKenna came into football relatively late in his life. A son of a farmer he was born across the Irish sea in County Monaghan, in May 1854 and like many of his generation, to use that awful phrase by Norman Tebbitt over a century later, he 'got on his bike' to look for work. He came over to Liverpool in his late teens and started work as a grocer's errand boy. But he soon moved on to work as a vaccination officer for the West Derby Union. It is most likely that it is here he first came into contact with Mr Houlding who was also a tireless worker for the poor of Liverpool. In this respect the pair had much in common.

He was a rugby man throughout his school days and while in the army he started the regimental rugby team and was a member of the West Lancashire Rugby Union. But it was around 1885 that he started to take an interest in football. He was persuaded to watch an Everton game, possibly by Mr Houlding, as the men had become friends by now through their work with the Union. He was in his late twenties at this time, but he took an instant like to the game and it was to replace rugby as the all consuming sporting passion in his life. It is no secret that when Everton first departed Anfield that the playing of rugby was considered at the stadium by Houlding as it was also gaining popularity in the country, but was still in its infancy too. Indeed the local papers of the day published a number of letters proposing such a thing. McKenna could have returned to the sport he turned his back on some years previously if Houlding had so wished, but the two rejected the idea and poured all their efforts into the creation of a first rate football team.

McKenna never shirked a fight and no doubt relished this challenge facing him with the departure or Everton. Moreover he spent his life fighting, but he would never have stood for an unfair fight. On the fateful night of the split and in the heated atmosphere of that meeting it came as no surprise to those that knew him that he would have sided with Houlding as the meeting was the culmination of a whispering campaign against Houlding with huge political undertones. The meeting was recalled in the excellent Bolton based sports paper of the day *Field Sports* by a reporter present as 'the most one sided meeting I have ever seen'. He went on to write that:

> When Mr Mahon, or Mr Clayton, or Mr Wilson desired to speak they were granted a respectful hearing from foes and friends alike, but every member of the opposition party was literally howled down, with the sole exception of Mr Houlding himself, whose weak voice and enfeebled state of health made it impossible for him to make much of an impression on the pre-conceived ideas of the majority.

There is no way that the straight talking McKenna could have let this pass. He himself was shouted down when he tried to interject. It is highly likely that his mind had been made up upon with whom to side in this unfortunate disagreement. But any lingering doubts were dispelled by the way in which the meeting was conducted and the way Mr Houlding was being treated.

The split from Everton left them with little as they moved to their new site and took with them the majority of the committee and playing staff. In a final insult the new Everton board tried to get Liverpool suspended from playing until Houlding paid for their new stands to be built. Initially they said they wanted to dismantle the stands at Anfield and take them with them as they belonged to the club, but Houlding had refused to sign away the stands. It was said at the time that Mahon wanted to leave Anfield 'a howling wilderness' but Houlding quickly sought an injunction from the courts to prevent any such act of vandalism until a proper hearing could adjudicate.

The FA committee listened at length to the arguments from the Everton delegation but ruled that they had no claim on Houlding's property as they walked out on the club after refusing reasonable financial offers. In a gesture of goodwill, and also to prevent the banning of football at Anfield with the start of the season just around the corner, Mr Houlding's son offered the Everton board the sum of £250, which they readily accepted with indecent haste, in return for an agreement they would not appeal or make any other attempts to sabotage Liverpool Football club from playing next season.

With the new club formed and registered with the Football Association there was still the small matter of having nowhere near enough players to form a team. Liverpool would have struggled to field a five-a-side team so the cunning McKenna was charged with the task of creating a team fit to grace Anfield in a matter of just three months. The affable Irishman set about the massive recruitment drive that was to form the basis of one of the most successful football teams in history—from scratch. McKenna targeted Scotland as a place he could find some talented guns for hire.

3

GUNS FOR HIRE

In the summer of 1892 McKenna wasted little time in assembling a crack team of mercenaries from north of the border. The aim was clear; Houlding wanted his club to become the biggest in Liverpool in order to get one over on the Everton turncoats he felt betrayed him so bitterly in the preceding months by dragging his good name through the mud. For his part, the brewer was busy with a share issue that would secure the financial future of the club and pay for the frantic recruitment drive that McKenna was on. The money making scheme would also fund the purchase of the ground by the club itself and mean it would be in control of its own future and never again could it be held to ransom by a few dissenting voices in the boardroom. It was the plan to grant the club independence from the meddling board members that the previous big wigs at Everton rejected before so the hard work and due diligence had already been carried out allowing him to set his bold plan in motion almost immediately.

He made the plan public as soon as he could, laying out his intentions for all to see and it was published in an editorial in the excellent newspaper of the day, *Field Sports*, as follows:

The prospectus of the Liverpool Association Football Club and Athletic Grounds Company, Limited, has been issued, and a perusal of it will leave no room for doubt to those who have a few loose 'quids' lying about their money boxes or stockings that they might do much worse than devote the said 'quids' to the promotion of good football and personal profit. At first sight the amount of capital (£15,000) may appear abnormal, but those intending to invest will see from the way in which the shares are issued and the considerations made by the vendors of the property that the risk is infinitesimal. In the first place the issue is confined to 5,000 shares of £1 each, to be called up in four amounts by 1st January next. Mr Houlding will sell the present ground, containing 13,600 yards, and Mr Orrell will sell the adjoining plot, containing 9,700 yards, for 7s 6d per yard, and adding to the amount for the purchase of these, the cost of all the fine erections, the total cost will be £9,237 10s. Mr Houlding has agreed to leave £2,700 on the mortgage of his land and Mr Orrell £2,300 on mortgage on his property, each at four percent, per annum, so that the purchase of the whole will be at once completed and a balance of £762 10s will remain as working capital. It is pointed out that if football and athletic sports are patronised as hitherto, the shareholders will not only be able to pay the interest on the mortgages (£200 per annum), but that £800 per annum will be wiped off the mortgages and sufficient money left for a dividend. Thus at the end of six years the shareholders will be in possession of a ground the capacity of which will form one of the finest enclosures in the country. It may be noticed that, unlike any other football ventures, which may be in the minds of our readers, the ground in this case will not revert to the original owners, but will be the absolute freehold property of the club for all time.

The short term result was to arm McKenna with a substantial war chest to lure the cream of Scottish talent into the professional game across the border during a very busy few summer months. McKenna knew he would have to work fast if he was to bag his prey as many English clubs had the same idea. Scottish players were highly sought after for a number of reasons. The game north of the divide developed almost independently from the English game and their FA.

The most striking result of this was the difference in the style of play. The football was based more on cooperation than brawling and charging, with the players preferring to pass the ball to each other in a bid to work the ball up field rather than just rush towards the goal with the ball in the freestyle manner of a Mongol horde as seen in sports like basketball today. Their scientific methods earned them the nickname of 'The Scotch Professors' because of their intelligent and well thought through moves. The papers of the time called their style 'combination play' and it proved to be quite successful against the free-for-all tactics of the English as cross-border games increased as the century went on.

On 30 November 1872 Scotland hosted England in what is now credited with being the world's first ever international match. A couple of matches had taken place in London in the previous years, but these were not officially sanctioned by the Scots and the side that represented them was made up of some exiles in the capital and their friends as opposed to players currently extolling their art in their homeland. The first match between these now famous old rivals took place in Glasgow at the West of Scotland Cricket Ground on Hamilton Crescent in Partick, for which the

Cricket club received the princely sum of £1 and 10 shillings rent for the day. Interestingly the game took place almost two years after the 'auld enemies' had clashed in a game of rugby. The hosts all played for Queen's Park, by far the biggest club in Scotland, while the English were a cosmopolitan bunch drawn from the likes of Barnes, Crystal Palace FC, Notts County, Wednesday FC as well as the university teams of both Cambridge and Oxford.

Just like in England, a football revival was in full swing in Scotland after years of suppression by the authorities and law makers of the land. The resurrection of the sport started a little later in Scotland, but by the 1870s their game was overtaking that of the English in terms of popularity and skill level at an alarming rate of knots. Celtic football folklore has it that a group of lads were said to be playing the game in Queen's Park, a luscious green space in the south of Glasgow and from there they went on to create the first formal club in the country.

'Tonight at half past eight o'clock a number of gentlemen met at No. 3 Eglinton Terrace for the purpose of forming a football club,' read the notes from the minutes of their first ever meeting at an unassuming terraced house on the evening of 9 July 1867. These were the pioneers of the game in Scotland. Their first games were against themselves or scratch sides that were thrown together as popularity grew. Not only did they supply the entire team for that first international, but they also supplied the kit. The players all used their dark blue club jerseys for the match, but with one difference. To note the significance of the match they had patches bearing the lion rampant sewn onto their shirts. These shirts have remained the same to this day. It must be noted that it was not the original intention to only play Queen's Park players, but the Scots were unable to obtain the services of two FA Cup finalists in Arthur F. Kinnaird of the Wanderers and Lt Henry Waugh Renny-Tailyour of the Royal Engineers who would have to wait another year to play for their country.

The Scots used a radical 1–2–2–6 formation of: Gardner, goal; Ker and Taylor, full-backs; Thompson and J. Smith, half-backs; R. Smith, Leckie, Rhind, MacKinnon, Weir and Wotherspoon, forwards.

For their part the English lined up with a more traditional 1–1–2–7 of: Barker, goal; Greenhalgh, full-back; Welch and Chappell, half-backs; Maynard, Brockbank, Clegg, Chenery, Ottaway, Smith and Morice, forwards.

The 2pm kick-off was delayed by some 20 minutes to allow the excitable throng of spectators to get into the ground. By the time the game started on St Andrew's day in 1872 the wintery sun had burned away the last of the lingering fog and exposed a glistening pitch that was still a little slippery underfoot as a result of the previous three days of rain that had fallen on the city.

But the dreary weather could not dampen the spirits of those who were treated to what was reported as an excellent game. Around 4,000 spectators had paid a shilling a head to watch the historic encounter between the two countries. The clash of styles was apparent from the start. The all-star English side was made up of a physically imposing bunch of bruisers and they took one look at their physically inferior opposite numbers and laughed. They expected the game to be a stroll in the park, literally, as they would be able to shrug off the Scots and bully their way to an easy victory. But they were in for a shock as the Scots bamboozled them with their relatively unheard of tactic of passing to each other to leave the English lads in their wake. It showed the limitations of their tried and trusted method of all their forwards hunting for the ball in a pack which was how the game had developed in all the public schools.

Their opponents had not gone through the English public school system and therefore came into the game with a fresh outlook which was to spread out on the pitch and pass the ball to each other as a team to disrupt the horde of English forwards. To their horror the southerners found their charging and barging had little effect as the ball had already gone before they sent their opponent sprawling in the mud. The result was that they were left chasing shadows for huge parts of the game as their slippery opponents ran rings around them. Intriguingly the match ended in a draw with neither side able to break the deadlock, although the Scottish fans thought they had the first goal just before the break when a shot from Robert Leckie flew narrowly over the tape that acted as a crossbar in these early days of the sport (wooden crossbars were not introduced until 1882 and nets a full decade after that). The result ensured there would have to be a replay to decide the bragging rights and started one of the keenest sporting rivalries in history.

The game acted as a wake-up call in England as their Scottish opponents drew many admirers from within the game and fans that saw the spectacle. This started the process of Scotch players making the trip south, but it was only a trickle to start with. The English sides were slow on the uptake and stubbornly stuck to what they knew rather than adopting the new fangled method of team play. As a direct result they were on the wrong end of some terrific beatings at the hands of the Scots and only won two of the first 16 matches between the two proud nations. The major change in their fortunes was intertwined with the advent of professionalism and the parochial actions of the SFA. Once the paying of players was now above board in England it was only a matter of time before the floodgates opened and the mercurial talents of the Scots surged south to make a living.

It was around this time that the representatives from the English and Scottish football leagues first met in an international fixture in Bolton. The match placed the best players of the two competitions against each other in front of 10,000 fans. It was a sign of the times that there were four Scots within the English league team and not one Englishman in the ranks of the Scottish league side. The crowd was swelled with scouts and officials from clubs all over England as they cast their eyes over the best that the Scots could offer and in the days afterwards the Scottish officials complained of their players being hounded with offers of work as the English clubs fought amongst themselves to secure the Scottish players. They were not alone as there were many Scottish managers doing the same thing away from the poisonous atmosphere of suspicion across the border.

It was no surprise then that the wise McKenna chose Scotland as the perfect place to find a readymade team to import to play on the hallowed turf at Anfield. Although his task north of the border was quite simple on the surface—recruit the best talent available and bring them south of the border. The reality was to prove rather more difficult as the anti-English campaign fought by the Scottish Football Association at the time was reaching fever pitch. The country was haemorrhaging skilful players to the riches of the English teams. Professionalism had not reached Scottish football officially yet and they were going through the same problems their English counterparts faced some years before.

At first the SFA tried to hold back reality by blacklisting players who were known to have turned professional in England. Put in simple terms, any players who went over the border would no longer be welcome to represent their country at any level. This deterred some, but had no real effect and did not stem the tide as the brutal reality was that playing for your country would not feed the families of the players as well as a career in England would. Lists of the banned players were posted around the country and are early testimony to the SFA's futile efforts to ignore a wider reality beyond their control.

Moreover, the SFA had to back down some years later as the national side started losing games as a result of having to play substantially weakened teams because of these petty actions. It was merely window dressing, though, because the great unspoken rule was that players based in Scotland would always be preferred to those in England wherever and whenever possible despite official protestations to the contrary. This pathetic practice was to carry on, although it was never officially acknowledged, for another century. Many gifted players were to miss out on international careers even relatively recently because of blinkered officials such as the inspirational Newcastle United skipper, Bobby Moncour, who only got a handful of caps throughout his excellent career almost 100 years after the ban had been officially lifted. Things had got so bad in those early years that by 1884 the banned list had over 80 names on it of players who had defected to England and each club had one or two Scots in their team. McKenna took this one giant step further with his recruitment drive. His team was taking on a particularly strong Scottish flavour.

There was, however, resistance from the Scottish clubs themselves as well as among some of the players who were split on the issue with some wanting to keep their amateur status and others wanting to turn the sport into a business. One thing that united the majority was that they saw it as only a matter of time before they followed their neighbours down the road to professionalism. A number of clubs set up 'Vigilance Committees' to warn off the scouts from the English sides that had come over the border to poach their best talent. It was great sport for the club officials and the newspapers clearly took pleasure in reporting the incidents of scouts having buckets of water thrown over them or being spotted and bundled out of grounds by officials.

Scouts for their part had taken to late night journeys to clandestine, midnight rendezvous with players in a bid to avoid the furious mobs organised by the clubs. For their part The SFA took a tentative step towards the inevitable by forming a league of their own in the same way the FA did some years before as a sop to the modernisers in the vain hope they could muffle the growing cries for professionalism. The same arguments raised their heads again as the spectre of match fixing was bandied around as the obvious result of paying players. But the King Canute-like stance of the SFA was flying in the face of what was inevitable to all but the most romantic within the SFA.

Their worst fears were confirmed as there was controversy when during the first league campaign St Bernard's FC were suspended by the Scottish FA for paying one of their players. It was clear that the football authorities were making an example of them to all the other clubs in a show of power and control. This row was not over and soon escalated when one of the biggest clubs of the day, Renton, played a friendly fixture against a team called Edinburgh Saints, which was in fact a thinly disguised St Bernard's team, and as a result found themselves expelled from the league's opening season by a very unimpressed SFA as punishment for consorting with the pay rebels. It was usual for clubs to supplement their league campaign with just as many friendly fixtures in order to boost their bank accounts. Renton's playing record in the league was expunged as the new competition was plunged into a deepening crisis so soon after its inception. It was also an act of sympathy on the part of Renton as they, like many others, felt St Bernard's were harshly treated.

Another unhappy episode surrounded three clubs who each had four points deducted for playing ineligible players in the 1890–91 season. The trio included some of the biggest teams of the day in Celtic, Third Lanark and Cowlairs. Renton successfully sued the SFA to have their suspension lifted following the St Bernards' debacle and subsequently resumed their place in the Scottish League for 1891–92. Despite the efforts of the SFA, like the FA before them in England, they could not prevent professionalism marching into the game and it was eventually adopted wholesale two years later. The powerbase in football had now shifted towards the clubs as it had done in the south previously.

* * * * *

This was of course no concern of McKenna's and he was certainly not deterred by any threats from the petty local militia as he always stayed on step ahead of the mob. McKenna used an agent in Scotland to do his scouting for him which enabled him to travel across the border already armed with a list of players he wanted to sign. It is rumoured that his friend and former Third Lanark player, Willie Maley, acted on his behalf as a scout and middle man. By this time he had signed for Celtic and went on to become their first full time manager in 1897 at the tender age of just 29 following a brief spell playing in England.

Pretty soon McKenna's first batch of recruits was gathering back in Liverpool and a lavish dinner was thrown to welcome them to the city at the Lathom Hotel. These players were now being prepared and trained in readiness for their inaugural season. A new training pitch and changing facilities had now been secured for the players to use. Mr Houlding had long wanted the team to have changing rooms of their very own closer to the ground so they did not have to use his hotel before and after every match. When Everton were still playing on their Priory Road pitch the team met in Everton Village, a long way from the ground and it was their board that approached Houlding and asked if the players could use the facilities at his hotel as a changing room and not the other way round as Mahon and his cronies had tried to make people believe. He consented of course and it was used as the club headquarters from that day on. Houlding for his part was pleased to help and picked up the associated costs for the use of his business premises without a murmur. And now with no hostile members of the board to veto his plans for their own ends he was able to rent the house at 27 Kemlyn Drive for the team to use. The back door of the terraced house adjoined the players' entrance at Anfield and the house had more than enough space for both sides to bathe and change on match days.

The Liverpool board were aware that the next step for the club was to enter the team into the league, but it was here that their plan to become the biggest team in the city hit the first of many obstacles. Teams were invited to join the league every season and a committee formed of various dignitaries from the clubs, league and the FA would gather and vote on which teams would take part in the competition that season. Liverpool duly handed in the appropriate form circulated by the league asking which members wished to make application to join the first division. The mood at the club was summed up perfectly by the following editorial comment in *Field Sports* on 4 April 1892:

> I am not in the least bit exaggerating when I say that the new Liverpool Association Football Club already bids fair to become a power in the land. Affiliation with the English Association is now a foregone conclusion and letters most cordially sympathising with the promoters of the new club have been received from some of the best known and most respected leaders of the Association football in this country. Moreover, the principal difficulty in all football clubs—that of finance—has been completely set at rest by Mr Houlding, who last week advanced the initial sum of £500 to secure players and to make other necessary arrangements, accompanying it with the distinct assurance that he neither expected or desired a farthing of interest upon his money; and further, that he should bear all the loss himself in the event of the undertaking not proving successful.

All hopefuls were also asked on the letter to leave themselves open for election for the newly formed second division should they not be successful in the vote for the top flight as places were limited to 12. It is here that someone at the club blundered as the clause on the Liverpool application had been struck out leaving application to the top flight only in a desperate bid to face Everton as soon as possible.

The league was not prepared to promote them straight into the elite division as they had not yet provided proof they had yet secured enough players to play a team of a high enough standard or that they would fulfil their full quota of games despite assurances from the club and the fact they had one of the best grounds in the country and financially they were stable thanks to the substantial wealth of Mr Houlding bankrolling the club.

The result was that they were left out of the league altogether and had to start in the local Lancashire League. There was more than a slight whiff of politics in the decision as the league also claimed Liverpool had been tapping up Alf Shelton of Notts County and as they took a dim view on it, the refusal could have been seen as punishment. The fact that Shelton approached the club himself as he knew they were recruiting only to be turned down flat by William Barclay after he contacted his opposite number at County made the decision even more incomprehensible. The Midlands club made it clear they had no idea the player was touting himself around to others and were not prepared to let him go so Barclay left it at that. The stuffed shirts at the league and the FA were still reeling from the drubbing from Suddell some years before and were not happy about the way Liverpool were going about assembling their side north of the border. The boycott by the league was more likely a warning shot to all the other Lancashire clubs they still eyed with suspicion to not follow Liverpool down the road of recruiting foreign players en mass. The FA were also showing their disapproval over the drawn out boardroom debacle that culminated with Everton moving, and therefore sided against the new club at the first opportunity.

This was more than just a minor set back despite the gloss the board put on it. Even though they were quick to point out to their investors and fans alike that one good season could see them into the second division and playing league football, while two successful campaigns would be enough to promote his club to the top flight where they would be able to compete head-to-head with his old club for the bragging rights of the city, the truth was they needed the crowds associated with the first division to fund the enterprise.

Nonetheless, the fact remained that the Liverpool board had messed up in the application and would have to take a massive financial hit in the meantime and hope that the team would prove an instant success. It is true to say that fans follow a successful side and although they would have fancied their chances in the league, they were producing a side that would match anyone in the Lancashire League. The proximity of the clubs in this lower division would also reduce their travelling costs quite significantly and the board could take solace in this. Undeterred by the news, the tireless McKenna continued his quest for a first class player for every position on the pitch with the same boundless enthusiasm although it cannot be denied that not playing in the top flight made the club less attractive to the players, but the club softened the blow by not dropping the amount of money they were prepared to pay the players for their undoubted talents. Around this time he turned his fire south of the border as he made a couple of raids on English clubs for more forwards with Jonathan Cameron arriving from Aston Villa and John Smith from Sunderland before heading back to Scotland to add the finishing touches to his now glittering squad.

As the summer of 1892 was in its full glory the new look Liverpool side was starting to take shape. Such was the confidence that the board had in the fruits of McKenna's labour that Barclay wrote a confident open letter to the press which read:

> We have joined the Lancashire League and have thus provided a very interesting series of fixtures for our team. We regret that we could not see our way to make the second division of the league as we felt, after careful deliberation that the gates would be no better than the gates we would get drawn with Lancashire clubs, whilst the travelling expenses would have been very high. We hope to meet some of the league clubs during the season and already engagements have been made with some of the leading Scottish clubs for odd dates. Cup ties— English, Lancashire and Liverpool—will fill up vacant spots and altogether I think the 'bill of fare' at Anfield will not disgrace the past. As to players the following have signed:—Sydney Ross, (Cambuslang) and played for Scottish League v Scottish Alliance; goal. Andrew Hannah (Renton), full-back. Half-backs; Kelso, (Renton), Cameron (Aston Villa) and James McBride (Renton). Forwards; John Smith (Sunderland), Tom Wylie (Everton), John Miller (Dumbarton) and Arthur Kelvin (Kilmarnock), and one or two men of less repute. In addition we shall have at least four of the best players in Scotland, with whom we are now negotiating. Our supporters

may rely on us that we will take the field with men who can and will play football and good exhibitions of the dribbling code will be seen at Anfield. Altogether our prospects are very bright and I anticipate a very satisfactory season on the old ground. Although we are the Liverpool club, all the old playing members of the old Everton, to whom Evertonions are much indebted for promoting the game in our midst, have been elected honouree life members of this club.

The missive was as much a clarion call of sorts to rally fans and ensure they came to Anfield when the season started as it was a statement of intent. Liverpool were competing for supporters with a well established and supported Everton side in the top flight and Bootle, now in the new second division, and faced the very real prospect that, as these two were playing league football, they could struggle to fill the ground of a weekend. They put their hope in the big name signings drawing the crowds as Suddell had done before with his 'Invincibles' at Preston North End. Fans in Liverpool already had the chance to see the current form of both Hannah and McBride in mid-April when they represented the Scottish League side that played their English counter-parts.

This was of no concern to the players who were being put through their paces. McKenna still had a few more surprises up his sleeve and so it was back to the tiny village of Renton that continued to punch well above its sporting weight and this time he returned with John McBride. Tough tackling half-back John McCartney was plucked from St Mirren, although he was to return to the club as manager, and Celtic provided the classy Joseph McQue to add guile to the midfield.

The team was pretty much complete and bolstered

74

by the addition of a couple of lads from closer to home who answered the following advertisement that was featured in a number of papers: 'The Liverpool Association Football club are determined to run a strong reserve team next season, and will be glad to hear from anyone with that object in view. Applications should be addressed to the hon. sec., Mr W.E. Barclay, 33 Everton-Terrace.' The ad gained them the services of Pearson from West Derby and William McOwen from Darwen, who, despite his surname, was in fact English. But McOwen fitted in well to a team now crowned 'The Team of all the Macs' by wags in the press because of the very heavy Scottish contingent.

Team building and training were now the order of the day with a new coach approved by the board to put the side through their pre-season paces. On a gloriously hot day in August the club held their first annual picnic and fun day. These events were quite commonplace at the time as a way for everyone at clubs to get to know one another and a very Victorian way to promote camaraderie within the club. Everybody involved at every level within the organisation, along with their families, took horse drawn wagons from the stadium for a pleasant ride across the Wirral to the beautiful Ring O'Bells Hotel on Village Road in the tourist hot-spot of West Kirkby where they disembarked and stayed for the day. During the afternoon and early evening various athletic events were arranged in the field next door to the historic pub which is said to have dated back to Norman times.

The role of honour was reported in the papers as:

100 yards flat race: Pearson, 1; Dick, 2; Berry, 3. Tug of war: Hannah's team, 1; Kelso's team, 2. 440 yards

race: McLean, 1; Jones, 2; Gilbert, 3. Long Jump;
Hannah, 1; Wylie, 2; McVean, 3. Hop, skip and jump:
Wylie, 1; McLean, 2; Dick, 3. 220 yards race: Jones, 1;
McVean, 2; Dick, 3. Dribbling contest: Miller, 1;
McVean 2.

After the exertions of the afternoon the club laid on
a substantial spread for tea during which prizes were
given out to the winners before they climbed back
into their carriages and returned to Anfield in the
early evening sun. These happy days were important
if the management were to bring together a
ramshackle collection of talented players and turn
them into a cohesive and effective team. This would
be essential if they were not to fall flat on their faces
in their first season.

There were many doubters outside the club who
still bore them ill will following the acrimonious split
of only a few months earlier and the wounds were
still raw. Indeed, some of the press were still carrying
on their spiteful campaign against the president of
the club which was borderline libellous and it
certainly would not have escaped court action today.
But Houlding, ever the proud man, remained
dignified in his silence and was determined to prove
to many that his new side were far more than just
the pub team made up of mercenaries they were
being portrayed as in some corners. Very soon he
would have his chance as the new season loomed
large. August was over as quickly as it started for
McKenna and his men as they knuckled down to the
hard work needed if they were to repay the faith
shown in them by Houlding.

Expectation amongst the fans was high as many
wanted to know just how this team of superstars
would gel together. Like an early version of the

Harlem Globetrotters, McKenna had gathered some of the best players available from Scotland for his team. The club organised an open training session at Anfield so the supporters could catch their first glimpse of the players.

Amazingly a full 6,000 people were reported to have turned up for the event. There was a buzz of excitement around the ground as the people who turned up talked amongst themselves about the relative merits of the squad. Many of these had very probably been regular supporters of Everton and now found themselves in the strangely familiar yet alien surroundings as their side had moved up the road. There must have been a few who were deciding if they should also move rather than watching the new team. Those that turned up felt a nostalgic pang when they saw the former Everton favourite Hannah run out on the pitch and gave the burly Scot a loud cheer as he trotted past them. An even louder roar of approval was heard when it was declared he would be captain for the season. McLean and Wylie were also warmly welcomed back to Anfield as the fans appreciated seeing their familiar faces again.

The first impressions of the fans were overwhelmingly positive as they liked the look of what they saw. The squad was divided in two and they played a short game against each other. Miller, Smith and Wylie looked as if they had been playing together for years with Miller scoring twice while Smith grabbed a third for his side. Ross also caught the eye in goal as he disrupted a number of attacks by fearlessly rushing off his line to smother the ball bravely at the feet of the forwards at the earliest moment. This was something new to the Liverpool fans and drew great applause. One early casualty was James Kelso who got his nose split open when the hard leather ball smashed into his face from close range and he spurted blood over the pitch and had to be removed for treatment. The phoney war was soon to be over as the long summer days were giving way to the fresh autumn mornings signalling the start of their first campaign was drawing close.

History was made on Thursday 1 September when Liverpool played their first ever game by entertaining Midland League champions, Rotherham Town, at Anfield. Bootle were originally pencilled in for this landmark fixture, but pulled out at the eleventh hour as it was feared by officials on both sides to be too contentious upon reflection. The stadium had been the home of the defending league champions only months earlier and therefore it was a disappointment to all concerned at the club when only around 1,000 people turned up to see this new side get started.

In an overcast, but warm, autumn evening the Liverpool players snaked out onto the perfect green baize of a pitch to take the applause of the few that had turned out. In amongst the crowd were a sprinkling of local dignitaries at the invitation of Houlding. These included the Mayor of Liverpool, Mr James De Bels Adam and new local Member of Parliament for the Everton district who remained in his post until his death in 1905, Mr John Willox. At just before 6pm skipper Andrew Hannah won the toss and started a great tradition that is carried on today. Liverpool's first ever captain chose to defend the Walton Breck Road end where the famous Kop grandstand was to be erected in 1906 to house their loyal fans and become the spiritual home of the club.

If there were any opening night nerves the players

soon got rid of them as they quickly settled and set about their opponents. The fans were behind their side from the start and their optimism was justified after only a few minutes before they were in front when Malcom McVean scored their first goal by thumping the ball past former Preston North End goalkeeper and legendary footballer, Arthur Wharton.

Wharton was born in West Africa in 1865 to a half Grenadian and half Scottish father and a mother who was reputedly a member of the Ghanaian royalty. He arrived in this country as a student and was to go on to become Britain's first black footballer after the talented athlete was spotted by various football clubs when he set a new world record for the 100-yard dash of 10 seconds at Stamford Bridge in 1886. Preston beat of a host of sides to his signature and he first played semi-pro with the Lancashire side in 1886 and was to make it to the FA Cup semi-finals in 1887 where they lost 3–1 to West Bromwich Albion. Wharton was considered by many within the game as good enough to play for England but he was never considered for the position by the FA, due in part to the racial prejudice of the time. He turned fully professional in 1889, when he signed for Rotherham United and was now the first goalkeeper to concede at Anfield to add to the other milestones in his excellent career.

It was soon to get worse for Wharton and his teammates as Liverpool continued the onslaught and added a second from the trusty boot of former Kilmarnock striker Arthur Kelvin soon after. One can only imagine what was going through the mind of Houlding at the time as he looked on from the stands as his team continued to score goals for fun. The fans were treated to a show-stopping performance from the familiar face of Tom Wylie. The former Everton man knocked in a spectacular first half hat-trick to send them into the break 5–0 up. While Liverpool were a bit of an unknown quantity before coming into this game, the Rotherham side would have been confident in the build up as they were well fancied by many to put in a strong defence of their title in the forthcoming season.

Harsh words must have been exchanged during the break as they looked a far better side in the second half, and they needed to be if they were to salvage anything from this game. With the wind at their backs they earned an early corner as they seriously tested the Liverpool defence for the first time during the match as they tried to fight their way back into the game.

But despite their best efforts there was no way that Liverpool were going to have their party spoilt and in Andrew Hannah and Duncan McLean they came up against a defensive brick wall. The two powerhouse defenders had answers for all the questions they were being asked by the Rotherham forwards and soon they were able to drive the back into their own half with a series of crunching tackles. Now that Liverpool were through the early sticky patch the game was soon flowing from one end to the other to the delight of everyone in the ground.

The visitors were now playing for pride and were determined to make a game of it and in doing so treated the fans to a breathtaking second half. Liverpool finished the stronger of the two sides and in the dying minutes looked by far the more threatening. The woodwork twice came to the rescue of Wharton before Kelvin added his second and

Liverpool's sixth with a powerful shot from the edge of the box.

If Houlding was rubbing his hands with glee after that goal then he must have thrown his hat in the air minutes later when John Miller announced his arrival in some style when he bagged a quite brilliant solo effort. The man crowned 'King of the Dribble' at the pre-season picnic, was reputed to be one of the most expensive signings that McKenna made, and he went some way to repaying the fee when the former Dumbarton man picked up the ball in the middle of the park and embarked on a mazy run towards goal. He danced his way through a number of tackles on his way into the box before placing the ball into the top corner with an inch perfect curling shot to send the crowd into raptures as they loudly cheered his classy goal.

With almost the last kick of the match the Rotherham team gave their fans something to talk about on the way home when they finally broke through the mean Liverpool defence to score a late consolation goal. It was a slight blot on the home side's copybook, but nothing more as the team had passed their first test with flying colours. Their clever build up play and short passing was typical of the Scottish way of playing and they did not look like a group of players who had only met a few weeks earlier. To a man they had impressed the curious onlookers who will have left the ground itching to tell their friends just how good they looked judging by the generous round of applause they received at the end of the game. But this was only a friendly match and there were to be much bigger tests on the horizon as they prepared for their league debut which was now just two days away.

4

THE LANCASHIRE LEAGUE

The morning of 3 September 1892 must have seemed like just the start of another rainy Saturday for the majority of people in the famous old port, but for everybody associated with Liverpool Football Club it was to be nothing short of historic as they kicked off their Lancashire League campaign against Higher Walton at Anfield. This was the culmination of all the hard work behind the scenes to get the club off the ground in the face of some fierce opposition. The players and officials expected the eyes of a whole city would be on them so had planned the day meticulously.

But, to paraphrase the famous old poem by Robert Burns, 'the best laid plans of mice and men often go wrong' and despite all the very careful preparations of the board, however, things did not start as smoothly as Houlding and the others would have wanted. For a start the 3.15pm kick-off had to be delayed by 45 minutes as the Higher Walton players were late, even though they had only a short journey from their base near Bamber Bridge. The formation of the league some years before had sought to stamp out this sort of thing which was commonplace only years before. Now that all clubs were affiliated the crowds had got used to games, not only going ahead, but also starting on time as both teams and fans knew the whereabouts of the clubs they were playing. In an unfortunate and mildly amusing error for all concerned, they had been taken to Everton's ground by mistake. Houlding brushed this off as being merely a minor blip that could not detract from what was to be a much anticipated debut. It was now out of the hands of Houlding, McKenna and Barclay and down to the newly recruited players who had only played together for a handful of weeks and were still getting to know each other in many respects.

The Liverpool team that lined-up for their Lancashire League debut took the familiar attacking 2–3–5 formation of the day. The early team line-ups were often split into two distinct halves. The perceived wisdom was that teams were broken down into a goalkeeper, five defenders and five attackers. This was quite typical of the time and the favoured one of almost all teams. The defenders would consist of both the full-backs and the half-backs. We would know these today as the defence and the midfield. The attacking five were made up of what we recognise as a pair of wingers and three strikers. It was certainly a far cry from the defensive formations we know today with a string of four defenders shielded by one or even two defensive minded midfielders playing the 'Claude Makele role'. This formation is so loved by the more un-adventurous managers of our time who let the fear of losing override their will to win and as a result produce downright boring sides in a hope to keep their job.

The Liverpool selection committee had chosen Sidney Ross to start in goal with the defensive pairing of Andrew Hannah and Duncan McLean sitting in front of him in their positions as full-backs. James

McBride, Joseph McQue and Joe Pearson were chosen as half-backs and were to patrol the midfield and act as a vital link when turning defence into attack. The forwards were Tom Wyllie on the right wing with Malcolm McVean playing as the inside forward alongside him, while on the left was Arthur Kelvin with Jonathan Cameron as company leaving John Smith stalking the area in search of precious goals. John Miller, who had scored such an excellent individual goal in the warm up match against Rotherham on the previous Thursday, had to watch the game from the stands having picked up a knock and was joined by fellow casualty James Kelso. Kelso was also sidelined through injury after having stitches when his face was split open in their first open training session.

Maybe because of the delayed start or perhaps as a result of the foul weather conditions, the game eventually got under way in a muted atmosphere around the ground. Both teams were given a warm round of applause when they entered the arena, but it was hardly the carnival atmosphere that the Liverpool bigwigs had been hoping for. There was only a disappointingly sparse crowd of around 200 or so wet-through spectators estimated to have been present on a bleak, blustery autumn day by the local press. These were the lucky few, though, as they were to witness what was to be a rip-roaring start to an eventful season for the club. Liverpool did not win the toss this time but they were again allowed to play towards the Anfield Road end of the ground in the first half as the Higher Walton skipper chose to play with the howling gale at his back from the kick-off. The powerful McLean introduced himself to the division with some early menacing challenges that soon put the opposition forwards in their place. The man mountain of a defender started as he meant to go on and his powerful performances were to be a feature of the season that the fans would come to delight in as much as the goals tucked away at the other end.

McLean, one of the few faces that the Anfield crowd would have instantly recognised as he played there with Everton in the previous seasons, was one of only two players who pinned their colours to Houlding's mast during the great split and turned his back on the majority of his teammates who marched like sheep to join Mahon at Goodison Park. The fiery redhead initially worked as a labourer during the week and turned out for Everton on the weekends after moving down from Renton in 1890. One of the biggest factors in his not leaving Anfield was the chance to be reunited at the back with his great friend and former neighbour Andrew Hannah.

McLean was his understudy at Everton before Hannah returned to Scotland to play with their home town club where the two first met. The departure of Hannah gave the young McLean a chance to shine as a first choice full-back at the club and now the two were given the chance to play together at last. Renton was one of the first stops for McKenna when he started his shopping spree north of the border and he must have desperately wanted to bring Hannah back to England to reacquaint the pair to devastating effect as the defender had been central to turning Everton into a championship side. A natural leader by example, Hannah would drive his teammates on throughout the game with his loud voice and fearsome tackling. He was an inspiration to those players around him from whom he would not accept second best on the pitch or off it.

It took a fee of £150 to secure his signature as well as the promise of a weekly wage of £5 during the season, according to reports in the newspaper *Scottish Sport*. This was a huge sum of money bearing in mind the top earners at the current champions Sunderland would have been receiving around £4 per week. The paper put the blame for such a good player moving away squarely at the feet of the SFA. 'One of the results of the refusal to grant professionalism will be, it is said, the departure of several of our noted players for the more remunerative south.' It thundered on 10 May 1892:

> It is more than whispered that Hannah, of Renton, is likely to be found amongst this number. It is said that he has again accepted an appointment in a Liverpool club at exceptionally handsome terms. £150 down and £5 a week have been quoted as the figures, which, if correct, is a complete justification for his relapse to professionalism. There are not many players who would scruple in these 'progressive' times, or would have the hardihood to decline such a windfall. The only matter for regret is . . . it will be a blow to Renton and a loss to Scotland. Hannah has, perhaps, done more than any of the 'old brigade' to recover Renton's laurels during the past season.

This broke the unwritten rule that had been agreed between the two associations that players should not be tempted by 'bribes' any bigger than £10.

Renton was an obvious stopping point for most scouts when they were in Scotland as they were one of the biggest sides in Scottish football at this time. Based in the footballing heartlands of Dunbartonshire, they hold the proud honour of being involved in the first official competitive game in Scotland. Although not original members of the SFA when they formed in the early months of 1873, Renton were one of the biggest driving forces in the formation of the league in Scotland and were able to play in the first ever Scottish Cup tournament later that year. On 18 October 1873 they were one of the clubs involved in the first day of competition for the new trophy when they took on Kilmarnock at a neutral venue at Crosshill, Glasgow, and ran out 2–0 winners. They kicked off earlier than the other two games organised for that day to write them into the history books as one of the first two teams to play a competitive game Scotland.

Renton went on to reach the semi-final that year, losing to eventual winners Queen's Park. The following season they went one step further, reaching the final, but again lost to the mighty Queen's Park, by 3–0. They did go on to lift the trophy in 1885 and they were once again to enter into the history books following their second cup win three years later when they faced the English FA Cup at Hampden Park in a challenge match billed as 'The Championship of the United Kingdom and the World'. Hyperbole aside, the glorified friendly would settle the bragging rights over who had the better sides—the English or the Scots on a typically terrible Scottish summer's day.

The date was 19 May 1888 and the game almost never got started as Glasgow was being ravaged by a terrible thunderstorm that was so fierce it had already taken the lives of four people. Not surprisingly the visitors wanted the game called off, just as predictably the hardy, West Coast lads did not, and in front of around 6,000 supporters they sent the English side back home empty handed after dishing out a 4–1 thumping. In truth it was about as credible a global trophy as the World Series in American baseball, but national pride was at stake—not to mention hundreds of years of antagonism and a few wars between the two old foes.

In the 1880s arguably the three best teams in the country, and therefore the world, came from a small area of Dunbartonshire; Vale of Leven, Dumbarton and Renton. So it was no surprise then that McKenna found rich pickings in this area. But by then they were on a steady decline as each of these towns, much like Cambuslang and many others of the day, were too small to support professional sides as they were home to only around 6,000 people and football was slowly drifting towards the big towns and cities. Without the crowd base to fund their newfound professional status they were forced to resign from the league only a decade after their 'world title' and the once proud side were eventually wound up in 1921 following an extended period in the lower echelons of Scottish football.

Although their years were numbered they produced many first rate players like McLean, a colossus of a defender who also became noted for his foraging runs into the opposition half after breaking up an attack and robbing the ball back for his team. While the fans loved to see him do it, the directors were less enthusiastic. In fact, one director famously scolded him in public when he wrote in the programme notes for a Cliftonville game in April 1893:

> Why will McLean persist in marring his really brilliant and effective play by getting too far away from his own goal? By all means back up the halves, but a full-back has no business whatever amongst the forwards, except on the defensive. If Mac will get rid of this one fault he will be as good a back as there is in England today.

The powerhouse defender was so complete a player that he was chosen as the club's penalty taker for the first season and scored six times in a total of 86 games for Liverpool. Not bad in a time when, as one of only two full-backs in the side, he was chided for venturing near, let alone past the halfway line. The best comparison to a modern footballer would be Stuart Pearce in attitude and stature. McLean also went on to earn two caps for Scotland once he moved back to his homeland in 1895 to play out the last days of his career with St Bernard's of Edinburgh, making his debut in a 2–0 win over Wales in March 1896. His partnership with Hannah was to prove key to the future success of the club as they provided a solid foundation for the side to build on.

Pearce's famously prickly manager at Nottingham Forest, Brian Clough, always claimed that the successful sides he had were built on a strong defence. And the fact that these two knew each other well must have filled the rest of this hastily put together band of brothers with confidence and now the Higher Walton forwards were about to be on the receiving end of their bone jarring challenges.

When the game eventually started with McVean kicking off, Liverpool were straight on the attack hoping to make their opponents pay for making them wait around thanks to their late arrival. The half-backs all got an early touch as they knocked the ball around amongst themselves in a bid to settle their nerves. The crowd were not given time to settle though as their pulses were soon racing after some great build up play down the left wing. The ball was poked through to McVean on the edge of the box and the striker swivelled and shot the ball just inches wide with barely a minute having elapsed in the game. Whether it was just nerves or simply a lack of communication there was what can only be described as a bit of a mix up in midfield between the anxious players. Their early touches clearly had not worked when Joe McQue and James McBride collided when trying to reach the resulting goal kick.

The cool head of Pearson came to the rescue as he kicked the ball out for a throw-in to the opposition before any serious harm was done. Harsh words were exchanged and as the situation threatened to escalate, Hannah stepped in and soon calmed things down. Through the intervention and encouragement of this wise old head the team soon settled and were able to focus on the job in hand.

But despite being a fairly new side and the shaky start to the game the Liverpool players soon hit it off. Smith and Wylie got their game going by exchanging passes expertly down the right wing. An early corner gave them a chance to put into practice one of their set piece moves they had rehearsed over the summer on the new training ground next door. The big men were summoned from the back to cause confusion in the opposition defence and it almost paid off as Hannah jumped highest to win the ball but his header was not on target and the ball skimmed the top of the bar and went behind for a goal kick.

Liverpool came even closer to taking the lead a few minutes later when a free-kick from McBride fell to the ever eager Smith in the box, but the former Sunderland man put his shot the wrong side of the upright. The home side had by now gone up a gear as they hunted for the opening goal. The Liverpool players were clearly determined to put a show on for their fans and when Smith ended a mazy run with a ferocious drive that was turned round the post for another corner the crowd were now right behind them following their blistering start. The slick move and shot encouraged the striker to try more and, with the help of Wylie, Smith soon started to show his class as the two produced clever inter-play as they probed the defence for weaknesses. It was plain to everyone in the ground that a player of the quality of Smith could not continue to miss if he was given the chances and sure enough he was rewarded with a thunderbolt of a goal on 15 minutes.

Cameron and Kelvin combined well down the wing to work their way cleverly through the Walton defence before intelligently sliding the ball through to Smith and the hitman did the rest. His clinical finish started what was to become a bit of a stroll for the home side. It was an excellent low strike, drilled into the bottom corner of the net that ended a superb flowing move and was a fitting way for Liverpool to score their first ever competitive goal.

Buoyed by their early breakthrough, the Liverpool players warmed to their task in hand and McBride, who had been drawing polite applause from the crowd with his tenacious tackling and pin point passing from midfield, doubled Liverpool's lead not long after.

The unfortunate Higher Walton goalkeeper did well to make a good save from Pearson, but was unable to hold onto the top corner-bound drive because of the ferocity with which it had been struck and the former Renton midfielder was first to react and pounced onto the rebound and hammered the ball into the empty net from the resulting scramble on the goal line. The home side were now well and truly on top and started to pepper the Higher Walton goal with shots despite having to battle against a howling gale and having the sun in their eyes. McVean, who had missed another excellent chance when he was again sent clear of the defence by Kelvin, soon made amends when he added a well taken third as Liverpool ran the Preston-based side ragged. This time he got his shot on target after escaping his marker yet again.

Not to be left out Cameron also got in on the act as he scored a fourth for the hosts. The powerful striker was in an uncompromising mood as he barged his way through the defence and the goalkeeper would have done well to see the ball let alone stop it when he thumped it past him and into the net. Higher Walton fought back at times, as you would expect, but their side had been weakened over the summer by some high profile departures and the Liverpool back line proved unbreakable with Hannah and McLean cutting every attack brutally short in a solid display of tough defending.

Despite the free-scoring, the star turn came not from one of the strikers, but from McQue who grew into his role as the game went on. Pretty soon the diminutive midfielder was controlling the entire game from the centre of the park with a superb display. The former Pollockshields amateur had made a name for himself with Celtic as a tough tackling midfield hustler with an eye for a defence splitting pass. Despite being small in stature he had the heart of a lion and a hunger to match. He was brought in by McKenna to add some steel to the spine of his side, but the Glaswegian was more than just hired muscle. McQue read the game better than most of his generation and this allowed him the rare ability of being able to dictate matches from the centre of midfield with his perfectly timed runs that enabled him to arrive late into a crowded box unmarked and his slide rule passing that could accurately pick out the well chosen runs of his forwards akin to a latter day Steven

Gerrard. He capped a brilliant performance against Higher Walton with a goal of his own just before the break when he ended one of his expertly timed runs with a bullet header as Liverpool cruised to a five goal lead at the interval with Pearson having already bagged the other to make up for being denied midway through the first half.

It was to be expected that the Higher Walton players would try to claw their way back into the game having had some much needed respite from the pounding they were getting from Liverpool on the pitch and to their credit they tried to play their way back into the game. Their purple patch lasted only a couple of minutes, though, as there is only so much inspiration you can find in the bottom of a cup of tea as Hannah and McLean continued their imperious form at the back and were able to repel everything that was thrown at them. It was always going to be a tough ask for the Higher Walton boys to turn this game around in the second half as they now also had some pretty horrible weather to deal with as well as a rampant Liverpool side that could smell blood and was driven on by the peerless McQue in midfield.

The Liverpool players were now queuing up to take pot shots at the visitor's goal as their defence crumbled in the face of the onslaught. McQue's passing left the Higher Walton players chasing shadows and never allowed them time to rest or catch their breath. Midway through the second half Cameron drew loads of cheers from the crowd when he scored his second of the match with a neat piece of dribbling to make some space for his shot before letting fly with a rocket from his right boot that soared into the goal. It was to their credit that the Liverpool players managed to sustain such a high level of sustained pressure even though the result was beyond doubt. Every second they had the ball would prove priceless in their development as they needed all the time together that they could get in order improve as a team. The goals kept coming and from the last of a string of three successive corners McQue was able to head home his second and Liverpool's seventh minutes before Smith fittingly completed the rout by ending the scoring spree he started almost an hour and a half before. The referee's whistle could not have come too soon for the Higher Walton players who were given a sound beating on the day at Anfield.

The home team dominated the game and ran out comfortable winners against a demoralised Higher Walton side by scoring eight without reply. One newspaper reporter of the time remarked it would have been more but for them 'having several of their efforts spoiled by the wind' and wrote that 'shots rained in like hail' on the Higher Walton goal while Ross had very little to do in goal thanks to the performance of the men in front of him. McKenna's summer spending spree looked good value as his side well and truly announced their arrival with this thumping of Higher Walton. Everyone at the club knew that tougher challenges would await them further on in the season, but this was still quite a dramatic marker to throw down and was a serious statement of intent. Anfield was recently home to the league champions and this side had a lot to live up to if they were not to stay in the shadow of their illustrious neighbours for too long.

Word had clearly spread around town about the exciting new team on the block and the number of people present for Liverpool's next home game numbered in the thousands rather than the hundreds. The match was a Lancashire Cup qualifier. The competition was seen as just as important to the fans as the FA Cup (or English Cup as it was known at the time) because not only was the final played locally and not in London, but also the best teams in the country were based in the county. As much as football fans complain about trips down to Wembley now, it was infinitely harder and prohibitively expensive for all but the wealthiest of supporters in the 1890s despite the massive expansion of the railways by the Victorians. The magnificent trophy was produced in February 1880 by the Bolton-based firm of Monk Brothers. The manufacturers had submitted a proposal for a most impressive cup standing a towering 39 inches tall and weighing in at about 175 ounces. The initial estimated cost for the trophy was £118, but this was later to be raised to £160 for the finished product. With the Lancashire FA at this time not being in the best state of health financially, several members of the Lancashire FA committee agreed to make personal contributions to help fund the purchase of the trophy.

Liverpool had been drawn against Southport Central in the first round and the expectation levels of the fans were now sky high after the way they demolished Higher Walton. Joe Pearson's removal from the midfield was the only change to the line-up as the excellent John Miller was ready to make his bow and it was the debutant who got the game underway. Both sides missed a string of chances to open the scoring in the first half of an end-to-end match that Liverpool slightly edged thanks to a combination of good goalkeeping from Ross in particular and some poor finishing from the

Southport front men. They were not alone in leaving their shooting boots at home as Miller had the chance to make himself an instant hero with the fans early on when he was picked out by another of McQue's trademark through balls, but his finish deserted him at the vital moment and he screwed the ball harmlessly wide of the post from little more than 12 yards out. While both sets of players were clearly putting in the effort neither could find that little something extra to unlock the opposing defence. The result was that the fans were still awaiting the first goal by the time the referee blew his whistle to mark the end of the first half as both showed more perspiration than inspiration.

Liverpool, though, saved their best football for the second half and were rewarded with the breakthrough when Kelvin turned the hard working Wylie's cross into the back of the net soon after the break with an excellent volley that left the goalkeeper no chance. Eyebrows were raised after the goal was disallowed to the annoyance of the home fans who let their feelings be known to the match officials in no uncertain terms as it was clear to everyone, apart from the referee, that the goal was perfectly good. The disgruntled fans did not have to wait too much longer for a goal, though, as Smith scored a comic opener minutes later with a speculative effort. His hapless namesake in the Central side completely missed his kick when trying to make a simple clearance and the ball rolled harmlessly into the back of the net. It was the sort of nightmare of a goal that goalkeeper's dread and will surely have kept him awake at night for some considerable time. If it had been scored today then it would have been a certainty for one of those cringe-

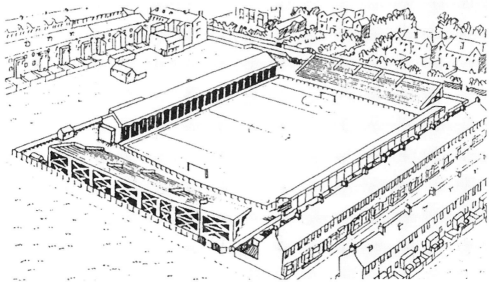

Anfield Stadium 1891

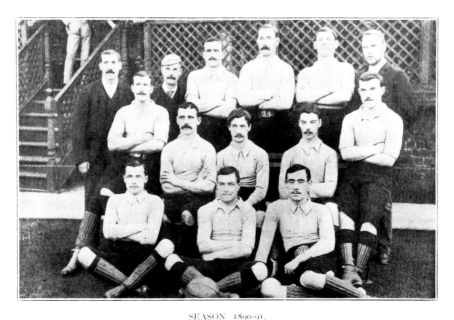

SEASON 1890-91.

D. WAUGH, *Trainer.* R. STOCKTON, *Umpire.* A. HANNAH, *Captain.* J. ANGUS. D. DOYLE. R. MOLYNEUX,
A. LATTA. D. KIRKWOOD. J. HOLT. W. CAMPBELL. A. MILLWARD. *Secretary.*
A. BRADY. F. GEARY. E. CHADWICK.

Everton FC team 1890-91, D. Waugh (Trainer), P. Jackson, A. Hannah, R. Smalley, D. Doyle, A. Smith, R. Molyneux (Secretary), A. Latta, A. Brady, D. Kirkwood, J. Holt, C. Parry, E. Chadwick, A. Milward, F. Geary

Image courtesy of The Everton Charitable Trust

Everton FC 1890-91. Andrew Hannah (back row, third from left)
went on to captain the new Liverpool FC team after the split
Image courtesy of The Everton Charitable Trust

George Mahon
*Image courtesy of
The Everton
Charitable Trust*

John McKenna

John Houlding

Liverpool team group: (back row of directors, l-r) J Dermott, B Bailey, S Cooper, FC Howarth, A Nisbet, H Cooper, C Gibson, HP Ellis, L Crosthwaite (middle row of players, l-r) John McCartney, Matt McQueen, captain Andrew Hannah, goalkeeper Billy McOwen, Duncan McLean, Douglas Dick, David Henderson, trainer F Whiteway (front row, l-r) Patrick Gordon, Malcolm McVean, Joe McQue, Jim McBride, John McKenna, President John Houlding, J Ramsay, Harry Bradshaw, Jimmy Stott, Hugh McQueen

Image courtesy of Press Association

J. McQUE,   J McCARTNEY.   A. HANNAH.   S. H. ROSS.   M. McQUEEN.   D. McLEAN.   J. McBRIDE   A. DICK (*Trainer*).
T. WYLLIE.   J. SMITH.   J. MILLER.   M. McVEAN.   H. McQUEEN

Liverpool FC 1892-93 season

Liverpool *v*. Newtown 1892

Cartoon illustrating Liverpool's 9-0 thumping of Newtown at Anfield in the FA Cup, 29 October 1892

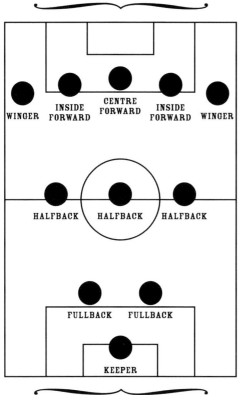

Illustration showing team formations from the period

Advertisements from the 1890s showing the 'new' equipment used at the time

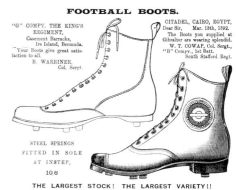

FOOTBALL BOOTS.

"G" COMPY. THE KING'S REGIMENT,
Casement Barracks,
Ire Island, Bermuda.
"Your Boots give great satisfaction to all.
B. WARRINER,
Col. Sergt.

CITADEL, CAIRO, EGYPT,
Dear Sir,   Mar. 18th, 1892.
The Boots you supplied at Gibraltar are wearing splendid.
W. T. COWAP, Col. Sergt.,
"B" Compy., 1st Batt.
South Stafford Regt.

STEEL SPRINGS FITTED IN SOLE AT INSTEP,
10 6

THE LARGEST STOCK! THE LARGEST VARIETY!!

FOOTBALL BOOTS, Laced to Toe Cap.
FOOTBALL BOOTS, Steel Springs in Sole at Instep.
FOOTBALL BOOTS, with Spring Heels.
FOOTBALL BOOTS, specially made Toes and Toe Caps, insuring True Kick.

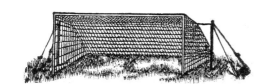

BRODIE'S PATENT ASSOCIATION FOOTBALL GOAL-NETS.

Per Set of Two Nets, with Steel Rope and Iron Pegs.
No. 5.—Strong Laid Hemp, Steamed Tarred...   ...   **35/-** net.
No. 1.—Very Stout Hemp, Steamed Tarred ...   ...   **45/-** „
Cheaper Fittings, ditto, not Steam Tarred ...   ...   **31/-** „
Carriage Paid.

N.B.—The above prices include everything except the actual Goal-Posts.

THE "REFEREE."

10/6   10/6

GAMAGE'S "REFEREE" MATCH BALL

ALSO RUGBY.   ALSO RUGBY.

Perfect in Shape, Welted Seams, Waterproof.
Every section stretched and hammered.
Price **10/6**, post free.
The "Holborn" **6/3**
The "Gamage" **7/6**

LIVERPOOL FOOTBALL CLUB

Ground: ANFIELD ROAD.

Authorized Programme and Fixtures.

ONE PENNY.] TUESDAY, 25th APRIL, 1893. [ONE PENNY

PRESTON NORTH END.

Referee—Mr. W. H. Gough.

Goal:
Trainor

Right Back: Left Back:
Holmes McGuire

Half Backs:
J Holmes Sanders Green

Right Wing: Left Wing:
Gordon Barton Becton Cowan

Centre:
Drummond

KICK-OFF AT 4 P.M. PROMPT.

Centre:
J Miller

Left Wing: Right Wing
H McQueen M McQueen T G Wyllie M McVean

Half Backs
J McBride J Cameron J McCartney

Left Back: Right Back:
D McLean A B Hannah

Goal:
McOwen

LIVERPOOL.

Match programme from Liverpool's game against
Preston North End, 25 April 1893
Image courtesy of the National Football Museum

John Houlding's former house on Anfield Road

The Sandon today

The Kop at Anfield 2011

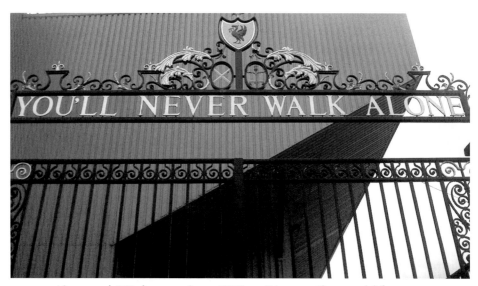

Liverpool FC's legacy since 1892 written on the world famous
Shankly Gates which were unveiled in their centenary year to pay
tribute to legendary manager Bill Shankly

worthy compilations of sporting errors narrated by one of yesterday's men that are Christmas stocking staples.

The rough-and-tumble encounter was hard, but fair. It was the kind of game that fans all delight in as two honest and hard working sides set about each other with purpose. McLean was an early casualty and was the recipient of some treatment after he dislocated his arm but was forced to carry on as substitutes were not to appear in the league for around another 75 years. The first recorded use of a substitute was on 21 August 1965 when Charlton Athletic's Keith Peacock, father to ex-Chelsea and QPR player Gavin, replaced injured keeper Mike Rose after 11 minutes of their match at Bolton. But McLean was built of sterner stuff—who could imagine any player today carrying on with such an injury when it seems a stiff breeze could take out some?

McQue again shone as he pulled the strings from midfield and was the focus of Liverpool's best play, but this was to be Miller's day. The forward marked his arrival on the scene with an excellent display of attacking football and the 22-year-old was unlucky not to be rewarded with a goal. His intelligent running off the ball created space for the rest of the Liverpool forwards to exploit. Tom Wylie benefited from his good play and added a second on the stroke of full time as Liverpool eased into the next round of the cup. Miller caused confusion in the Central defence as Liverpool broke from their own half with the ball. The forward took his marker out wide with him and allowed Wylie to cut inside to the gap where the defender should have been and clip the ball over the advancing keeper and into the net to put the result beyond any doubt.

The end of the month meant a return to the league, only this time it was against some well fancied opposition. Liverpool were to face their first stiff test in the shape of the previous year's double winners, Bury. The much fancied side from Greater Manchester took home the Lancashire League and Cup trophies and were going to provide the first decent yard stick for the team to gauge themselves against and would give the 4,000 or so fans who turned up, including around 500 noisy supporters who made the trip from Bury, a better idea of what this new team was all about.

The opposition were well fancied to finish the season as champions again by many. They were a well oiled attacking machine and strong in every department. To win the Lancashire Cup the previous season they beat some very good sides that they were not really expected to turnover including, as many of the new breed of Liverpool fans will have recalled, Anfield's former side Everton. They also silenced the big guns of Bolton Wanderers before putting Blackburn Rovers to the sword in the final for an improbable win to all but the most one-eyed of Bury fans. In the league they stormed to the title by securing an incredible 40 of the 44 points available. It was during this successful campaign they are said to have earned their unusual nickname 'The Shakers'. Before the final on 23 April, legend has it that the Chairman, Mr J.T. Ingham, was being questioned about his team's ability to beat the supposedly stronger opponents that day by some fans and he is said to have replied 'We shall shake 'em. In fact we are the Shakers' and that the supporters adopted the phrase as a rallying call to their team.

The Liverpool committee decided to bring James Kelso, whose brother, Bob, played for Everton and then Preston North End, into the side to make his first, and only, league appearance due to the absence of John Smith through injury, but the backbone of the team remained the same. The teams lined up as follows:

Liverpool: S Ross, goal; A Hannah and D McLean, full-backs; J Kelso, M McBride, and J McQue, half-backs; T Wylie, J Cameron, J Miller, M McVean and A Kelvin, forwards.

Bury: Lowe, goal; Baugh and Warburton, full-backs; Pemberton, Jobson and G Ross, half-backs; Wilkinson, Spence, Clegg, Bourn and Plant, forwards.

Hannah won the toss for the home side and with the kick-off set for 4pm he made the early leaders of the league, Bury, face the last of the late afternoon sun for the first half. Bury, like Liverpool, were still unbeaten and as expected attacked from the kick-off with a view to stamping their authority on the match early on, but the Liverpool back line was again well marshalled by Hannah and McLean. The pair had to be at their best in this game as they were facing an unbeaten side that had scored 14 goals already and only conceded twice so far in all competitions. The home side weathered the early storm well with Ross being called upon to make two splendid saves early on. Wylie gave the home fans early hope when he jinked down the right wing and, after riding two particularly heavy challenges from Baugh and then Warburton, expertly he tried his luck from distance and he sent a curling shot dipping narrowly over the bar and behind for a goal kick. That was as good as it got for Liverpool as the visitors had by far the better of the opening exchanges with Clegg and Bourn both coming close to opening the scoring. These were desperate times for the Liverpool defenders as they had to withstand wave after wave of attacks from the visitors. Bury, though, failed to get a goal despite their early dominance thanks mainly to the fact that Ross was in breathtaking form in goal. His fisted clearance of a Clegg free-kick was so impressive that it in fact drew applause from both sets of fans.

Liverpool continued to cling on and once the Bury players looked to have punched themselves out they eventually started to play their way back into the game thanks to another terrier like performance from McQue. The midfielder turned defence into attack superbly by never letting the opposition settle on the ball and dictating the play masterfully. Even in the most one-sided of games the team under pressure will always get a chance to break and perhaps score. It is just a case of patiently hanging on and so it was that as the half wore on the home side grew in confidence and eventually got into their stride.

With 10 minutes left before the break it was the turn of the home side to hit top gear with Kelvin coming close when he tried his luck after cutting in from the left wing. Although his shot flew over the bar it gave the fans a chance to voice their support for their club. Liverpool, roared on by their supporters, eventually made the visitors pay for their wastefulness in front of goal by taking the lead late on in the first half through the relentless Miller with a well crafted goal. The forward had been linking up well with his wingers throughout the game and left Lowe in the Bury goal no chance with his well placed shot after some deft work from Wylie and Kelvin down the right touchline. Kelvin received a ball thrown out by Ross and the pair worked their way up field to fashion an opening. Once the pair made it to the by-line the ball was fired across the face of the goal from Wylie to Cameron who, in turn, cut the ball back to Miller for a simple finish in the six yard box.

Bury fought back as expected, but again the Liverpool defence creaked a little but was never broken by the defending champions. Things got better for McKenna's men when they made it two soon after. Again Wylie was the architect when he ended another of his trademark runs down the right by setting up Cameron to score his third of the season with an excellent finish. Liverpool were not only winning but they were now playing some brilliant football as well.

The Bury players were clearly shaken themselves as they had not played badly, but they found themselves two goals down. Things very quickly got worse for them when McVean added a third a minute later with a thunderbolt from outside the box that rattled the underside of the bar as it flew into the goal. As the Bury players re-started the game following the second goal the ball was robbed by McQue and put into the path of McVean. The home side were now fully in control and lay siege to Bury's goal. It was the turn of the Bury players to face an onslaught. Wylie came close to doubling his tally for the season with an effort that sailed narrowly over the bar and would have been just reward for his incisive runs down the wing, but it was Miller who all but ended the game as a contest on the stroke of half-time when he tucked away his second and Liverpool's fourth. The striker ended a bustling run with a powerful finish before saluting the home fans who could hardly believe what they were seeing as the home side hit four goals without reply in a 10 minute goalfest.

Bury had their chances to score in the second half with Hannah having to head one shot off the line when Ross was eventually beaten, but their attacks were against the run of play and it was as much as Bury could do to stop Liverpool adding to their tally in the second half and the home side ran out 4–0 winners to put them second in the table with a game in hand on their table-topping opposition.

The score was a fair reflection on the game as Liverpool recovered from their nervy start to completely outplay their esteemed opponents. The only player to come out of the game with any real credit on the side of the defending champions was their goalkeeper. The fact that Liverpool did not get to double figures was mainly down to Lowe. The result was to send a shockwaves throughout the league and sent a message to the rest of the teams in the division who still had any doubts that Liverpool meant business this season. This Bury side were expected to steamroller the new side and maintain their unbeaten start to the season, but Liverpool out-gunned and outsmarted them in every department for a hard fought, but well deserved victory.

The *Cricket and Football Field* of 1 October reported the win under the title of 'Liverpool Larrup Bury'. This win was all the more remarkable because the Bury side were said to be better than the one of the previous year that won the double with such ease. What impressed the crowds and reporters alike at the match was the style of the win and flowing football they produced. This was no smash-and-grab victory but a confident and stylish display. It was described as 'pure and perfect football, nothing else' in the paper. Liverpool were fast becoming the talk of the football community with many wanting to see just how long their run would last. Most commentators were expecting their challenge to falter in the winter months and saw their good start as a flash in the pan, beginners luck, because even a broken clock tells the right time twice a day and many within the city were still expecting time to be called on their promotion charge very soon.

Lancashire League up to Saturday 21 September 1892

	Pld	W	L	D	F	A	Pts
Fleetwood Rangers	3	3	0	0	12	4	6
LIVERPOOL	2	2	0	0	12	0	4
Blackpool	2	2	0	0	5	1	4
Bury	3	2	1	0	8	6	2
South Shore	2	1	0	1	10	6	3
Fairfield	3	1	1	1	7	10	3
Heywood Central	1	1	0	0	6	1	2
Liverpool Caledonians	2	1	1	0	4	4	2
Nelson	3	1	2	0	7	9	2
Rossendale	2	0	2	0	2	6	0
Southport Central	2	0	2	0	2	4	0
West Manchester	2	0	2	0	4	12	0
Higher Walton	3	0	3	0	3	19	0

5

A FAMILY AFFAIR

September turned into October and with it came a turn for the worse in the elements. Next up for Liverpool was the first instalment of a double header against a West Manchester side who had not had the best of starts to the league. This was not to say that they were push-overs, but Liverpool were again at home and the confidence was now coursing through the veins of the players in blue and white halves (Liverpool did not adopt their ruby red shirts of now worldwide fame until 1896).

The game was originally to be played away, but the venue was changed because of the state of the opposing pitch and now Liverpool played hosts in truly terrible weather. The howling wind and rain ensured the most difficult of playing conditions for both sides and was to prove to be a great leveller as Liverpool's slick passing game would be heavily hampered on the sticky surface. The switch also meant the crowd was not as big as would normally have been expected, but there was an upside to this as those that did turn up could all take advantage of the excellent Anfield facilities and shelter from the awful weather under the covered stand that caused so much trouble a year before. The return of Smith up front for the home side meant there was no room for Cameron in the forwards and he was pushed back to midfield at the expense of Kelso.

West Manchester lined up with Entwistle, goal; Sugg and Russell, full-backs; Spiers, Pickering and Allison, half-backs; Bridge, Iddon, Bogie, Walsh and Leigh forwards.

The two were drawn to meet in the Lancashire Cup only a week later and, as so often happens in football, their league encounter fell on the Saturday before the cup tie. This was an opportunity for either one of the sides to get a handy psychological advantage over the other ahead of the cup showdown. The game was an end-to-end affair as neither side could take control of the match because of the heavy pitch. The weather was proving harder to tackle than the opposition.

The first real chance fell to the visitors when Bogie took the ball down the left wing and sent Bridge clean through with an exquisite pass that turned the otherwise solid defence. But Hannah was quick to realise the danger and managed to make up a huge amount of ground to get across to make an outstanding last ditch tackle in the greasy conditions as Bridge was shaping to shoot. Smith was clearly hoping to make his return to the side a permanent thing and showed early promise, having a couple of early efforts saved as did his fellow forwards Miller and Kelvin in a dramatic five minute spell during the first half.

The home crowd thought they had taken the lead on 25 minutes when Wylie ended a jinking run with a powerful drive that beat the outstretched Entwistle only to ripple the wrong side of the side netting. To one half of the ground it looked as if the ball had gone in, but their celebrations were cut short by cat calls from the rest of the fans. West Manchester gave as good as they got throughout the game and tested the Liverpool defence with a series of attacks and even won an impressive string of six corners in row. But the home defence stood firm and despite the best efforts of both sides in an entertaining start to the game the tempo dropped quite dramatically after half an hour. As the ground underfoot deteriorated to resemble the Somme it was quite understandable that the game descended into a war of attrition in midfield as the pace with which they started was clearly unsustainable. The result was that neither side was able to take control of the match and it remained goalless at the half-time break despite the best efforts of all concerned. The visitors did have one last hurrah just before the whistle went in which they forced a couple of dangerous corners and only Walsh will know how he did not manage to score when the Liverpool defence made a complete hash of clearing the second of these and he sliced the ball wide when presented with an open goal.

The visitors started the second half the way they ended the first and caught Liverpool cold after the break. The home side found themselves one down almost immediately after the re-start when Bogie picked up the ball and made a bustling run to the by-line before cutting the ball back to Bridge who neatly side-stepped a desperate lunge from Hannah and fired the ball past the despairing Ross. The goalkeeper was furious because it was the first goal they had conceded in a competitive match. His despair, mixed with a few choice words from skipper Hannah, stunned the rest of the side into action and like a wounded animal they fought back ferociously. The fans were almost treated to a goal immediately as Liverpool were a whisker away from drawing level just a minute later when Wylie skimmed the top of the crossbar with a sizzling effort that would have ripped the net if it had been on target.

The home side were now well on top and were running rings around the opposition, but they could not convert their domination into goals. But they refused to let their good start to the season be ruined by a momentary lapse of concentration and although they left it late they did eventually get back on level terms through Wylie. The former Rangers man eventually got the breakthrough when he thumped Kelvin's teasing cross into the net after McVean slalomed his way through the West Manchester defence to loud cheers from the crowd as the clocked ticked away.

McVean was fast becoming a favourite of the crowd as they marvelled at the runs he first became famous for at his previous club—Third Lanark. Third Lanark are the fondly remembered, scarlet shirted club from the south side of the city now part of Scottish football folklore. The club have always been regarded as everyone's second favourite team in the football mad city of Glasgow. The Third Lanarkshire Volunteers were founder members of the Scottish League, and won the championship in 1904 and the Scottish Cup in 1889 and 1905 (beating Celtic and Rangers respectively). Also known as Third Lanark, Thirds, the Warriors, and the Hi-Hi, the club hit hard times after the Second World War and were relegated from the Scottish First Division in 1965, losing a spectacular 30 of their 34 matches and ending up with a miserly seven points. Within two years the club was declared bankrupt and thrown out of the league, eventually being wound up soon after. It was a sorry end to a once proud club, but the memory of the club lives on to this day as they have taken on a cult status amongst football fans with many visiting the site of their former ground Cathkin Park. After being wound up in the courts the land has been turned into a public park in the City and the council preserved many of the old features. A natural bowl of a ground and the large mud banks of terracing can still be found amongst the trees as can the famous old pitch where the players plied their trade. Fans of the old club and members of the public alike can now stand on what was once the pitch and dream of what it was once like for players like McVean to torment opposing players with his mazy runs.

His good work was the catalyst for Liverpool's comeback against West Manchester and signalled the start of a goal frenzy from the home side that their opposite numbers could do little about. Smith made it two soon after when he poked the ball home after a frantic goalmouth scramble as both sets of players fought tooth and nail to get the ball.

With their spirit now broken the Liverpool players pushed for another and were rewarded when Miller added a classy third with a minute to go. McQue picked him out with a pin-point lob over the defence which he ran onto and, after checking his stride, smashed the ball goalwards with an emphatic volley from just inside the box and although Entwistle in the West Manchester goal managed to parry his shot, the former Dumbarton man had the reactions of a cat and was first to the rebound and fired the ball into an empty net as they came from behind to wrap up an exciting win with three goals in the last 15 minutes.

The score was perhaps a little harsh on the visitors

as they will have probably thought they should have earned a share of the points and had they not tired significantly towards the end of the match could well have done so. But successful league campaigns are built on winning games despite not playing well or controlling games. All top sides continue to fight until the final whistle which was the most outstanding feature of Sir Alex Ferguson's modern day Manchester United side. His side had a reputation for scoring late goals, none more so than in the 1999 Champions League victory over Bayern Munich, but that was not luck. Every side he produced fought like a dog with a bone until the very end of the game. That is the mark of true winners and one that McKenna's side showed in the way they continued to believe until the final minute of the game.

The victory was sweet, but the West Manchester lads soon had the chance for revenge as the two sides met the following Saturday in the final Lancashire Cup final qualifying round at their dilapidated Brookes Bar ground. The stadium was in such a poor state that the Liverpool team put in an official protest to the match officials upon their arrival, this was later withdrawn, but nonetheless it was an indication of the unsuitableness of the ground for a high profile match.

The league match a week earlier had been switched because of concerns from both clubs that the pitch would be unable to handle two games in quick succession because of the heavy rain that had fallen in the previous few weeks. Another concern for Liverpool was the state of the dependable McLean who had damaged his arm during a midweek 6–1 defeat in a friendly at Glasgow Rangers and only passed a late fitness test on the morning of the match. But such was his steadying influence on the team he started the game and played much of it without moving his arm for fear of damaging it further. Again Liverpool ran out 3–1 winners with Miller scoring twice before Kelvin got his first goal for the club to see them safely for the first round of the competition where they were to face Darwen in the new year.

There was still no return to the league as first was the small matter of the FA Cup. Fans knew the winners of the historic competition were the best team in the whole country as the early years included Scottish sides too. The first winners of the competition were The Wanderers of Battersea—one of the greatest of all the early Victorian teams. They played in the first final which was held at the Kennington Oval where they beat Royal Engineers by a single goal. The Engineers, formed in 1862 under the captaincy of Major F. Marindin, were an army club and were to feature many more times in the history of the competition as they were beaten FA Cup finalists in 1872, 1874 and 1878, and winners in 1875. They were credited as one of the first English sides to adopt a team approach to the game as many clubs moved away from a rolling maul towards what we would recognise today. The Wanderers, for their part, went on to win the trophy another four times before professionalism and the rise of the northern clubs consigned them to the history books.

Kennington was chosen for the early finals because it was one of the few wide open spaces that would be able to handle the large crowds that football was now attracting. The final was to be played there for all but one of the first 22 years until this season when it was to be played in Manchester. A year later the competition was to be held at Goodison Park before returning south to Crystal Palace until 1915. The huge venue at Crystal Palace (no relation to the current football club) was perfect for the final. The structure was originally a glass and iron construction built in Hyde Park to house the great exhibition of 1851 in which the Victorians put on a show to flaunt everything that was good about this country and the empire to the rest of the world. After the exhibition the building was carefully taken down and rebuilt in south London so the public could still roam around its great halls as a leisure pursuit. Parks with manmade lakes boasting water features such as fountains were all the rage in the Victorian era and this venue boasted many. The cost of keeping such a place running was proving too much as the years went on and one of the lakes was filled in to cut costs.

The result was a perfect pitch that caught the eye of the FA and it was agreed that Crystal Palace would host the FA Cup final for two decades after 1895. Another trip to Manchester followed before Stamford Bridge played host for three years until Wembley Stadium was opened in 1923. Originally named the Empire Stadium, Wembley replaced a smaller running track that had been on the site since the 1880s and was to go on to become synonymous with the competition after the first final, known as the 'white horse final' in which huge crowds turned up to watch Bolton Wanderers beat West Ham 2–0, endeared the competition to the public.

The famous old competition was the way that clubs judged who should be crowned the best side in the country as the league was still in its infancy and did not include any of the London clubs. Teams had to apply for permission to participate and were invited into the competition prior to the season starting. The competition boosted the coffers of all those who took part, but this season had an extra incentive as the FA had agreed that from now on the runners-up would be given commemorative medals, not just the winners.

Liverpool's first game in the world's oldest knock out competition was a trip to Nantwich on 15 October and a late 10 minute goal spree from John Miller, who hit a quickfire hat-trick, eased them to victory after Wylie had opened the scoring with 20 minutes left in the match as they once again left it late. Their belated goal glut was in keeping with a game that started half an hour late because the referee, Mr Turner, missed his train and had to wait for the next one. More amusingly was one of Miller's goals which proved to be a talking point among the fans because of its comedy value.

The match was played in torrential rain that showed no signs of stopping throughout the 90 minutes. As the game was nearing its conclusion the pitch had been steadily cutting up due to the almost biblical downpour to the point that the Nantwich goal became a bog. Miller's shot stopped dead on the muddy goal line and both he and the home goalkeeper raced towards it for opposite reasons. In the ensuing tussle, as both players wrestled each other to get the ball, neither could quite reach it as they rolled around together in the mud. It was only when the referee blew his whistle and rushed over to pick the ball up before placing it in the centre circle that anyone realised the ball had crossed the line. The home side, for their part, made a game of it, but they missed all their chances and so were dumped out of the competition. Liverpool were safely through to the next round thanks to their late flurry of goals.

A return to the league on 22 October brought about the return fixture at lowly Higher Walton who had been leaking goals at an alarming rate as they had been on the end of some sound beatings since the two last met. The visitors kicked off and the problems in the home defence were there for all to see when Miller opened the scoring with Liverpool's very first attack. He neatly tucked away McBride's cross as they got off to the perfect start.

The home fans must have been fearing the worst when McVean broke clear of their defence in the next attack only for his blistering drive to bounce back off the crossbar with the goalkeeper well beaten. The majority of the rest of the half was spent in the Higher Walton half with Ross only being seriously tested once during the half when he made a terrific save from a Parker pile-driver. Liverpool continued to probe and to the credit of the home defence they succeeded in frustrating their opponents until a minute before the break when Liverpool eventually managed to double their lead with Miller again the scorer. McCartney ended a powerful run by picking out Miller in the middle with a perfect cross that he nodded home with ease bringing to an end the stubborn resistance of the Higher Walton team.

While it is not possible to win a league championship in the first few games of the season it is possible to lose it during this period and there was much to admire in the way Liverpool had started their campaign and the spirit the team was showing.

By contrast, the poor opening to the season by Higher Walton had seen them only pick up the one point with a draw at home to South Shore and end any realistic hopes they had in the title race. Liverpool, for their part, were flying and had only conceded one goal in their 100 percent start. Moreover, they did not look like leaking any more in this game against inferior opposition. The ever impressive Miller secured his hat-trick soon after the re-start and Wylie chipped in with a well taken pair as they swept Higher Walton aside scoring five goals without reply. While that was an end to the scoring, things got worse for the home side as they had to finish the game with 10 men after Forest suffered a gash to his leg following a full bloodied challenge by the powerful McLean. Unfortunately for Higher Walton they were fast becoming the whipping boys of the division having now conceded a whopping 33 goals in six matches—over twice as many as the next worst defensive record held by West Manchester. But teams can only play the opposition that is put in front of them and it surely would have been a terrible mistake for Liverpool not to heap more misery on this side while they were struggling for form and confidence.

Liverpool ended the month with a return to the FA Cup and a second round qualifier at Anfield resulted in an emphatic win over a well fancied Newton team that had no less than five Welsh internationals in it at the end of October. The Liverpool squad had been significantly strengthened by the arrival of the highly rated brothers Matt and Hugh McQueen who had recently signed from Scottish side Leith and were to make their first appearances for their new team over the border. Matt, the younger of the duo, was brought into midfield while his brother played up front. These two were to provide the finishing touches to the team as their undoubted skill added much to the side. It could have been so different for the Welsh side had they taken their early chances, but their wastefulness in front of goal was ultimately to cost them dear.

McCartney, having made his debut in the previous round of the competition, opened the scoring with his first goal for the club after a delicious lob over the Newton keeper who had a habit of straying off his line in a bid to beat the Liverpool forwards to balls over the top of his defence. His plan backfired badly thanks to the quick thinking of the former St Mirren man. Wylie added another with a fine effort from the edge of the box that curled in off the post and claimed the third, although it looked like an own goal by one of the Newton defenders, Townsend, as the two tangled while trying to reach a dangerous low cross at the near post.

Newton were sinking fast as Liverpool dished out a lesson in passing football to them. With just a few minutes left in the first half McVean got another to send Liverpool into the break with a comfortable four goal lead. Wylie had another shot ruled out that he hit so hard that it did actually burst the net and nestled outside of the goal after hitting the advertising hoardings. The referee assumed the ball must have gone past the wrong side of the post and gave it as wide. There were howls of protests from the Liverpool players but the official was not going to be swayed by the appeals of the Scots and awarded a Newtown goal kick to re-start the game.

That was the only piece of luck Newton had as the day was to get worse, much worse, for the visitors after the break as McKenna's Liverpool side ran riot. McVean and Wylie soon doubled their tallies after half-time before Hugh McQueen marked his debut with a well taken goal to make it 7–0. Wylie went on to add another for his hat-trick before Cameron made it nine without reply from the visitors to the delight of the thousands of fans who loudly cheered Liverpool off the pitch after such a resounding win. The 9–0 score-line may have suggested an easy day out for the Liverpool players, but the empathic result raised eyebrows amongst players and fans alike from the other clubs in the competition because Newtown were not considered to be a weak side at the time.

It would be easy to suggest that perhaps the Welsh side were having an off day, but commentators on the sport at the time suggested the arrival of the McQueen brothers was the missing piece in the jigsaw at Anfield. Scottish papers were full of surprise that the duo, not only had chosen to sign for Liverpool given the amount of interest the two had generated amongst the biggest sides of the day, but also over the low key way in which the club marked winning the race for their signatures.

Hugh was perhaps the better well known of the pair as his marauding runs down the left wing often caught the eye, but it was his crossing that earned him the respect of his teammates. It is said that the older McQueen could not just pick out a player with unnerving accuracy, but that he would joke with players in training about being nice to him or he would make sure the laces on the ball would be facing them for their header making it a far more painful experience than would otherwise be the case. The fun loving winger was said to have come close to death while at training at the club. The whole side were taken to Southport swimming baths to work on their fitness. Legend has it that McQueen had to be dragged off the bottom of the pool and out of the deep water after diving in off the springboard only later to reveal to his startled teammates that he could not in fact swim. The pair could not have wished for a better introduction to the English game than the comprehensive thumping of Newton. The next round of the cup, though, presented them with a tricky tie away to Northwich Victoria in the middle of November.

Following the drubbing of Welsh side, Newton, came a top of the table clash as Liverpool travelled to the Royal Palace Gardens, as their Raikes Hall ground was better known, to face a strong Blackpool side. McKenna's side had comfortably beaten everyone they had come up against so far. West Manchester held the honour of being the only side to have managed to score against them in competitive football while at the opposite end the forwards had helped themselves to a stunning 38 goals in the eight league and cup matches they had played so far this season. But in Blackpool on bonfire night in 1892 they were to face a much sterner test of their abilities than they had faced in all competitions with the fireworks coming from the home side.

Blackpool had undergone many changes of their own over the summer as they brought in a number of new faces themselves to beef-up their squad and in Lal Wright they had one of the best goalkeepers, certainly in the division, and possibly the country. His impressive displays meant that the Seasiders had also yet to drop any points and had only conceded three goals themselves in their unbeaten four league game run. The three sides shared top spot coming into the game, but the impressive goal difference of 20 for and only one against put Fylde side second with Bury in third as the Manchester side had played two more times and suffered two defeats. Something had to give if one of these two clubs were to extend their perfect starts to the campaign and draw clear at the top. Both Bury and Blackpool fought tooth and nail for the title last season with the former winning by five points in the end. The pair were expected to do the same again this season with little opposition, but Liverpool had well and truly crashed their promotion parties and now had to be considered as serious players in the division. They had come from nowhere and turned the Lancashire League into a three horse race.

The match was billed as Lancashire against Scotland by the local papers in Blackpool as the visitors included no less than nine players who had played north of the border recently in a bid to whip up the crowd in the build up to the match. The preparations for Liverpool were disrupted just minutes before the start of the game when McBride had to withdraw from the team after being taken unwell on the journey to the ground and was replaced by Joe McQue, himself carrying a knock from the last game. Liverpool were also without Smith, their talismanic goal machine, who had still not recovered from an injury picked up in the 3–1 victory over West Manchester at the start of October.

The teams lined up for the eagerly awaited encounter as follows:

Blackpool: S Wright, goal; E Morgan and H Parr, full-backs; F Parr, H Davy and H Stirzaker, half-backs; J Parkinson, H Tyrer, W F Marsden, J Pittaway and E Parkinson, forwards.

Liverpool: S Ross, goal; A Hannah and D McLean, full-backs; J McCartney, M McQueen, and J McQue, half-backs; T Wylie, J Cameron, J Miller, M McVean and H McQueen, forwards.

Liverpool won the toss, decided to kick-off and were forced to play into the wind and the sun for the first half. Their first attack ended in a goal kick to Blackpool and that was almost the closest they came to scoring for the rest of the half because the home side started like an express train and were on the attack as soon as the referee from Halliwell, Mr Lomax, blew his whistle to re-start the game from the goal kick. Morgan controlled the clearance expertly and sent Parkinson down the right channel with an inch perfect ball and he forced a corner off Matt McQueen that the Liverpool defence only just managed to scramble away. There was a look of panic amongst the Liverpool defenders as they had yet to experience an onslaught like this. The Blackpool blitzkrieg had taken the visitors by surprise and in the next attack it was all McLean could do to put the ball out for a throw-in with a last ditch tackle to stop E. Parkinson from scoring. It was only a brief respite as the striker scored from the resulting throw-in with a spectacular effort from the edge of the box that gave Ross no chance in the Liverpool goal.

It very soon got worse for Liverpool as they found themselves 2–0 down with not even 10 minutes on the clock. J. Parkinson picked out Pittaway with a perfect cross and the striker made no mistake by shrugging off the attentions of Hannah before banging in the second with his head. Blackpool were making a mockery of Liverpool's hitherto excellent defensive record with two goals in three minutes. The home side were now rampant as the partisan crowd roared them on for more. The fans could not have dreamed of such a good start and were in full voice with the noise almost deafening. The pressure within the stadium was steadily building and soon told with a second strike from E. Parkinson giving Blackpool a three goal lead before half-time after Hannah was caught in possession inside his own half. Liverpool had improved as the half went on, but they never really looked like getting one back before the break so complete was the domination by the home side. The best they could muster was an effort from Wylie that flew over the top of the bar.

McKenna was a man to be feared and respected in equal measure and no doubt the Liverpool players were dreading what he had to say to them during the break. He was a gentleman soldier who became a member of 4th Brigade of Artillery Volunteers, rose quickly through the ranks and soon achieved the position of Sergeant Major. He was immensely proud of his time with the army and enjoyed its regimented ways. He was remembered by those he served with as being a strict disciplinarian—'a man of action' was how one soldier described him.

His stern words in the visiting dressing room clearly had been taken on board by the players as his side produced a far better performance after the break with Liverpool eventually putting the ball in the Blackpool net. Their celebrations, however, were cut short as the goal was ruled out for a handball in the build up. This was not to be their day despite their best efforts. Wright was in inspired form in the home goal and produced a number of fine saves to break the hearts of the travelling fans. It was starting to look as if their side were never going to score and their worst fears were confirmed when Miller ran with the ball from his own half and sent Cameron through on goal only for the striker to fluff his lines. In searching for a way back into the game Liverpool had to be careful not to leave themselves open to conceding more as Blackpool were a constant threat.

The Seasiders were able to soak up all that was thrown at them before launching a stinging counter-attack themselves. Their comfortable win could have been more but for another good game from Ross who was the pick of the visiting players. Not content with the Blackpool players testing him, Hannah almost put the ball into his own net under pressure but his blushes were saved by a smart stop from Ross who managed to push the ball around the post while at full stretch.

Liverpool were undone in the first half an hour of this game and never really recovered their composure enough to look like getting anything from the game until the final 20 minutes. The forwards were not given a second to think by the home side as they pressed and harried whenever they lost the ball to good effect with Harry Parr looking like a world beater at the back. Miller never really got the supply from his fellow forwards to have a real impact on the match, while in midfield McCartney was reduced to persistently fouling his opponents as they dashed past him. There is no doubt that Liverpool finished the game the stronger of the two as McQue and Matt McQueen saw a bit more of the ball, but the damage had been done early on and left them too big a mountain to climb. Their lightning start to the match was enough to earn Blackpool the points and inflict the first defeat of the season on an under-strength Liverpool team. McKenna's side now faced a long trip back to Anfield to lick their wounds and reflect on the footballing lesson they had just been taught by one of the pre-season favourites for the title. The result saw them lose a little ground at the top as Bury handed out a 6–1 pasting to their near neighbours Heywood Central and leapfrogged over Liverpool into second place.

Lancashire League up to Saturday 5 November 1892

	Pld	W	L	D	F	A	Pts
Blackpool	5	5	0	0	14	3	10
Bury	7	5	2	0	27	12	10
LIVERPOOL	5	4	1	0	20	4	8
Fleetwood Rangers	4	3	1	0	14	6	7
South Shore	5	1	0	4	18	14	6
Liverpool Caledonians	5	2	1	2	11	8	6
Fairfield	5	1	1	3	10	13	5
Rossendale	5	1	3	1	11	15	3
Nelson	5	1	3	1	12	17	3
Higher Walton	7	1	5	1	7	33	3
Southport Central	5	1	4	0	6	10	2
Heywood Central	4	1	3	0	10	15	2
West Manchester	4	0	3	1	7	17	1

6

FA CUP HEARTACHE

The defeat to Blackpool was a blow to the side, but damage to the confidence of the players was soon repaired when normal service was resumed a week later as Liverpool got back to winning ways with a 4–1 thumping of Blackpool's Fylde neighbours, Fleetwood Rangers on a beautiful November day. Their opponents had done little recruiting over the summer as they were deemed to have a decent enough squad of players to finish better than their third place in the previous season. But they were found wanting by a rampant Liverpool side looking to banish the memories of the pounding they received at the hands of Blackpool.

McBride and Smith were welcomed back into the side as McKenna wanted his team to get back to winning ways quickly. He demanded a performance from his team to make up for the loss and he was not let down as Miller opened the scoring with a fine effort early on in the first half. But their lead did not last long as Fleetwood equalised from the kick-off with a scorcher from distance that fizzed past Ross. It marked a purple patch for the home side in which they came close to taking the lead on three occasions. Despite the ferocity of the fight back Liverpool held their own and soon were back on top themselves. They had spent the whole week seething at their first defeat and there was no way they were going to suffer another loss so soon. A quick-fire brace from McVean sent them into the break with a deserved 3–1 lead. Rangers were better than the score-line suggested and showed why so many tipped them to be the team to challenge Bury and Blackpool for the title in the second half as they tried to get something out of the game, but a captain's display from Hannah kept them at bay. The Liverpool skipper had one of his finest displays for the club as Rangers were a constant threat through their mobile forwards, but the brilliant McQueen brothers caught the eye as they showed why so many clubs had been chasing them. The returning Smith wrapped up the win with a fourth in the second half which broke the fighting spirit of the plucky Fleetwood players as Liverpool warmed up for their FA Cup match against Northwich in style. Fleetwood had to face high-flying Blackpool in the second round of the competition and on the evidence of this display could not have been looking forward to the prospect.

Liverpool's FA Cup game against second division side Northwich proved to be a highly controversial affair. It was the final qualifying phase before the big teams were to enter into the competition in the next round. The officials at the club protested about the very fact that the game was going ahead as they thought the substandard pitch unplayable. Heavy rain had been falling for days on end in the build up to the fixture and in a bid to get the pitch playable so the tie could go ahead the grounds men at Drill Field, so named as it was the former drilling ground of the 22nd Company of the 3rd battalion of the Cheshire Rifle Volunteers, had put huge amounts of sawdust down. The result was to turn the playing surface into a boggy mess with large pools of water sitting on top of a sludgy quagmire of soggy wood chippings and swamp-like mud. The protest had as much to do with money as it did with the pitch as the Liverpool board were also keen to switch the match to Anfield as their ground could hold many more fans.

The Northwich board turned down their substantial offer of money to change the venue and pressed for the tie to go ahead as scheduled knowing full well their best chance of winning would lay within the confines of their small ground and to play away at Anfield would make their chances of progressing into the draw for the next round much harder. In return the visitors tried one last time to get the game called off by using the obviously poor, but nonetheless playable, pitch as an excuse.

It was not the only skirmish in a phoney war between the chiefs of the two clubs desperate to get into the first round proper and a potentially money spinning tie against one of the biggest clubs in the country. Liverpool's preparations for the game were dealt a blow with an enquiry about the eligibility of the impressive Matt and Hugh McQueen, who had stolen the show a week earlier against Fleetwood, as there was some doubt as to whether they were eligible to play in the competition due to the date of their registration for the club. McKenna had no choice but to leave the two out just minutes before the kick-off while the matter remained unresolved and play the game with a weakened side. He was confident the two could play, but he could not take the chance and risk the side being thrown out of the competition. The replacements, Joe McQue and Arthur Kelvin, were perfectly good players in their own right, but they were not quite of the class of the brothers McQueen.

Despite all the goings-on behind the scenes the

game did finally start on time and the home side kicked off. No doubt reeling from the late changes to the team and the disruption to all the careful planning that the late inclusions must have caused, Liverpool did not start well and were given an early scare when the home side almost scored with their first attack, drilling the ball into the side netting with the visiting defence all at sea. Liverpool rode their luck in the early stages and even found themselves a goal up against the run of play. Tom Wylie showed his marker a clean pair of heels down the right wing, cutting inside and curling the ball delightfully towards the top corner, but Gow in the Vics goal managed to get a hand to it and start a game of pinball in the box as players from both sides ran in to reach the rebound. The ball eventually found its way back to Wylie who was on the edge of the scrum of bodies and he made no mistake the second time and blasted the ball in from 12 yards before wheeling away in delight.

Miller almost made it two 10 minutes later when he was sent clear of the defence by McVean only to lose his footing as he tried to steady himself to shoot and slipped over in the mud amongst howls of laughter from the home fans. The pitch was making passing difficult and both sets of players resorted to a long ball game to avoid the ball sticking in the middle of the park. The result was that the game became frantic and both teams had chances to score. Hannah and McLean both produced goal saving tackles at the back while at the other end Smith looked for a minute as if he was the only player on the pitch with studs on his boots when he twisted and turned his way through the defenders and left them in his wake only to be denied at the end when a heavy touch allowed Gow to dive at his feet and smother the ball.

Northwich eventually got themselves an equaliser just as the game looked to be slipping away from them. Liverpool seemed to have the measure of their opponents and were slowly getting on top when Fecit struck for the home side. The diminutive forward slipped between Hannah and McLean to be the first to reach a curling cross from the right wing and volleyed the sodden ball into the back of the net in spectacular fashion to send the home fans into a frenzy of hope just as their team looked as if they were going to be bundled out of the competition.

If that was unexpected then what followed must have been a real shock to the system for Liverpool as they soon found themselves 2–1 down. Again it was Fecit, although this time the goal was far less low key as he managed to poke the ball behind the line from a goal mouth scramble, but it was greeted with delirious joy from the home fans that could now sense victory over their non-league opponents. The gloves were off and Liverpool abandoned any notion of the passing game as they fought like lions to get back on level terms. The fast and furious pace showed no signs of letting up as half-time approached as Wylie, Miller and Kelvin all had chances the score in an absorbing encounter.

Liverpool had a real fight on their hands if they were to stay in the competition and sure enough they came out with all guns blazing in the second half. The Northwich players barely touched the ball in the opening 15 minutes as they were treated to an exhibition of passing football from the visitors. Wylie came closest to getting his side back on level terms when his drive from the edge of the box clipped the top of the crossbar and flew over on the hour. But despite laying siege to the Northwich goal, McKenna's men could find no way through. They moved the ball around the pitch well and probed for a weakness with their possession play but to no avail. The home side weathered the storm and played their way back into the game as Liverpool looked to have punched themselves out. Both sides created chances to score more goals in the last half an hour of the game and McKenna's men thought they had done enough to earn a replay late on after Miller pounced onto a weak back pass that held up in the mud and scored only to have his effort wrongly ruled out for offside as the referee thought it was a Liverpool player that put the ball through and not a defender.

The Liverpool players and fans alike were furious with the outrageous decision that cost them a legitimate goal and could have earned them a hard fought replay at Anfield, but referees never have, and never will, change their minds once they have made a decision so the score remained the same until the final whistle. Spurred on by a sense of injustice, Liverpool threw everything they had into attack in the closing stages of the match and missed more chances to score in the last minute in a fiercely contested and incident packed end to the game. It was a bitter first defeat for the club in the competition and one that would have been very hard to take for the board in light of all the shenanigans in the build up. Liverpool had enough chances to deliver an upset in the competition, but a poor pitch and even worse decisions by the officials conspired to send them out. Although their first flirtation with the FA Cup was only to be a brief one, it was to prove as dramatic as it was limited.

The swapping of venues for FA Cup matches in return for financial inducements was not uncommon. In fact Liverpool's next opponents in the league, Rossendale, did that very thing that weekend when they accepted the princely sum of £80 to surrender home advantage to double chasing Bury. The fact they went on to beat the well fancied Bury side made them instantly famous within the game and gave them great heart while preparing to take on McKenna's promising side at their lofty Dark Lane ground. McKenna went into the game still without the McQueen brothers as Scotland international Matt was best man at his older brother Hugh's wedding on the day of the match.

Phillip Kelly was drafted in to make his debut as a forward and almost made himself an instant hero with the fans when he was gifted an early opportunity to stake his claim for a regular place in the side, but he missed an absolute sitter which would have given Liverpool an early lead. Wylie and Smith were combining well down the right wing to keep the home side under constant pressure as Liverpool tried to burst the bubble of confidence surrounding the Rossendale team pre-match after their FA Cup success. McCartney put in a great shift in the midfield and along with his tenacious tackling he was dictating the play with accurate passing. This was a much improved performance from the midfield dynamo. But despite their best efforts they failed to turn their dominance into goals before the break. For their part the home side saw little of the ball, but they did have the best chances of the half. Ross had to make three brilliant saves to keep his side on level terms. With half-time fast approaching Wylie had the best chance of the game so far when he used his pace to get round the back of the Rossendale defence and pick up a long through ball from McLean but his shot, although on target, lacked the power needed and was easily cleared.

It looked to be a case of 'as you were' after the break as the pattern of play seemed to be following that of the first with Liverpool dominating possession but lacking the cutting edge on the final third. The game was crying out for some individual brilliance from a player to get the opener—and Miller provided it. Liverpool got a magnificent goal midway through the half when Miller and striker McVean combined for one of the goals of the season. The pair one-two-ed their way up the length of the pitch without any of the Rossendale players even close to getting a touch of the ball before Miller added the coup de grace by ending the flowing move in spectacular fashion.

The Rossendale players looked on helplessly as the dynamic duo left them chasing shadows in their wake. His goal was greeted with mild applause as the disgruntled Rossendale fans begrudgingly acknowledged the exquisite play they had seen. Had the goal been scored by one of their own then they would have been quite rightly shouting their name from the roof of the stands. But it wasn't. The home side were well and truly second best in the game now, but they still created chances and following a rare miss-kick from Hannah, Ross pulled off a superb save to keep his team in front and served as a timely reminder to the Liverpool team the game was not yet safe despite their showboating.

McVean and Kelly both missed chances to secure the game before McBride eventually added a well taken second to give them some breathing space in the match by catching Holden, the Rossendale goalkeeper, off-guard with a clever, quickly taken free-kick that he fired into the goal. The home side finished the game by far the stronger of the two sides, but were unable to apply the finishing touch to their fine build-up play.

Liverpool ran out deserved winners over the entire game, but the fact they did not concede in the last 20 minutes was as much down to luck as stout defending and brilliant goalkeeping from Ross. If someone had walked in late he would not have believed that Rossendale were the side that were losing. In fact, in the dying minutes they looked far more like the side that hit seven past Bury the week before, but the two were not scheduled to meet until the following March so they would have to wait months before being handed a chance to get revenge.

Back in the winning groove, Fleetwood were the next visitors to fortress Anfield as Liverpool welcomed back the excellent McQueens to their line-up. The Liverpool board were still furious over their exit from the FA Cup and the supposed ineligibility of the two brothers. William Barclay was due to attend a regular FA meeting in London later that week where he was planning to kick up an almighty fuss over the affair. But first was the small matter of the return match against a Fleetwood side that looked to have improved in the meantime as they started the game in quite an assured manner. They faced the same Liverpool side that had beaten them 4–1 only three weeks earlier and kept Liverpool at bay for most of the half before they conceded the opener. The writing was on the wall for them as Wylie was making mincemeat of the visiting defence down the right wing and had fired couple of shots over the bar before setting up McVean for the first goal.

And worse was to come for the Fleetwood team as the Liverpool Juggernaut was simply revving its engine and a quick-fire hat-trick from the prolific Miller gave Liverpool a surprising 4–0 lead at half-time that soon put paid to the early optimism of the Fleetwood fans and dismissed any thoughts that they could contain this impressive side.

Miller was not happy with just the three and scored another when he headed a hanging cross into the box from Hugh McQueen into the net. Liverpool's sixth and Miller's fifth followed minutes later when Smith broke through the Fleetwood defence with some determined running before crossing the ball off to his 22-year-old strike partner who again used his head to great effect inside the box. Matt McQueen made it a magnificent seven when he opened his account for the club with a thunderbolt from midfield and wrapped up a superb win. This took them back to joint second spot on the same points as Blackpool and just two points off the top but with a couple of games in hand on the leaders Bury.

This season was Miller's one and only with Liverpool as he left at the end of the season to join The Wednesday (who would later go on to become Sheffield Wednesday) after scoring 27 goals in 28 games, including three hat-tricks. His five goal haul ensured he would be written into the Anfield history books as only four other players, Andy McGuigan in 1902, John Evans in 1954, Ian Rush in 1983 and Robbie Fowler in 1993, have managed this feat in competitive games. Before joining Liverpool the likeable striker ran the line for his former club Dumbarton while negotiations between the two clubs took place so he could still help out his teammates while not risking an injury that would stop him turning professional and moving to England. His spell south of the border only lasted a few years before he returned to Scotland and played out the remainder of his career with Airdrieonians.

His astonishing performance set up the visit of the Seasiders to Anfield on 17 December very nicely indeed. So keen was the interest as these two locked horns that the local reporters of the day estimated this to be the biggest crowd of the season so far as around 6,000 fans crammed into the ground to watch the match and roar on their respective teams. Both sides put out their strongest XI to add to the air of a showdown for the title. Liverpool had come through their midweek trial without picking up any injuries as they had a break from the league campaign and warmed up for the game with a 1–1 draw with Heywood in a friendly fixture to keep the players match fit and earn much needed funds to keep the club on an even keel. Even though the season was not even halfway through, the match was seen by many as the decider for the championship— although the Bury side will surely have had something to say about that. Blackpool named the same starting XI that had run McKenna's men ragged in the first game while Liverpool included James McBride for the industrious Joe McQue and John Smith came in for Jonathan Cameron.

The teams were:

Liverpool: S Ross, goal; A Hannah and D McLean, full-backs; J McCartney, M McQueen, and J McBride, half-backs; T Wylie, J Smith, J Miller, M McVean and H McQueen, forwards.

Blackpool: S Wright, goal; E Morgan and H Parr, full-backs; F Parr, H Davy and H Stirzaker, half-backs; J Parkinson, H Tyrer, WF Marsden, J Pittaway and E Parkinson, forwards.

In the first match Liverpool were undone by the high tempo with which Blackpool started the game and never recovered enough, spending the majority of the game on the back foot. Blackpool kicked off, but conscious of the way they opened the previous encounter, the Liverpool half-backs soon robbed them of the ball and it was the home side that were first to settle down and missed a host of early chances to take the lead with Wylie, Miller and McQueen all coming close to opening the scoring.

The crowd were in full voice before the match and urged on by the bright start to the game by the home side. Despite promising much in the opening exchanges Liverpool could not get the early goal they desired and the visitors managed to hold off wave after wave of Liverpool attacks. The visitors, known as the 'Merry Stripes' because of their fluid attacking style and their blue and white striped kit, always looked dangerous on the counter-attack and eventually hit Liverpool with a classic sucker punch when Pittaway ended one such breakaway with a well taken goal to open the scoring. The move started with a Liverpool corner that ended in a melee in front of the goal. The ball was eventually hacked away to Parkinson who skipped past the lunging tackle of McLean before sending the ball into the box and Pittaway applied the finish. The goal stunned the crowd who had been treated to 10 minutes of constant Liverpool pressure, but now found themselves a goal down against the run of play. The finish, as well as they way in which they managed to thwart all the early attacks from Liverpool, invigorated the visitors and they hit a purple patch of their own after the goal and both Hannah and McLean had to produce goal saving tackles to keep their side in the game and stop Blackpool running away with it.

Marsden had the pick of the away side's chances

when he ended a strong run with a powerful shot that Ross found too hot to handle and McLean managed to hack away under pressure from Pittaway who had followed the shot in like all good strikers should in case of a rebound. With half-time approaching the Liverpool players had regained their composure and once again set about methodically breaking down the opposition and creating chances by passing their way through the Blackpool side. No matter what they threw at the visitors, though, they could not crack their defence.

Both Parr and Morgan were playing brilliantly at full-back and on the few occasions they did get through the human wall of a partnership Wright looked a world beater between the sticks. With only minutes left the Liverpool fans thought they were back on level terms when Wylie managed to cut in from the wing and jinked past Wright in the Blackpool goal, but inexplicably he missed the target with the goal gaping. To make matters worse Smith did exactly the same with the last attack of the half and left the Liverpool fans scratching their heads over their half-time pie as to how they were not on level terms.

The home side rallied during the break and Miller had their best chance of the match soon after half-time when he brilliantly dribbled through the Blackpool defence only to be denied at the last by some desperate defending from Parr as he was about to pull the trigger. The crowd roared their approval of his play, but they had little else to cheer about as the game was put beyond Liverpool soon after when Blackpool got their second through a long range effort from Marsden that caught Ross by surprise. The striker sold the normally reliable Hannah a dummy on the edge of the box before releasing a snap shot that flew into the top corner.

Blackpool were clearly a team built more on perspiration than inspiration and it was perhaps a little fortunate, but it was always a danger while the Liverpool forwards were squandering all their chances at the other end. The home side could not be faulted for their lack of effort in trying to salvage something out of the game with Wylie denied on a couple of occasions by some excellent saves, as well as some huge slices of luck, by Wright in the Blackpool goal who put in a man of the match display.

The 'keeper acknowledged the warm applause of the crowd after one such save when he nudged a curling shot onto the post with his fingertips only for the ball to bounce back into his hands rather than the path of the incoming forwards during his impressive performance by removing his cap to take a bow and revealing a completely bald head for which he received no end of friendly banter from the Liverpool fans in the stands.

McBride and Hugh McQueen were both denied by Wright in the dying minutes as Liverpool threw everything they had at Blackpool, but despite the best efforts of the home side this was to be Blackpool's day as they held on, somewhat fortunately it has to be said, to their lead and took both points. The defeat meant that Blackpool had now done the double over Liverpool and caused much speculation amongst the press and the fans alike about the validity of their title credentials and their position as co-favourites in the eyes of some to top the league in their first attempt. The fact that Blackpool had now completed home and away wins over McKenna's team was compounded by the fact they had failed to score in either tie even though they boasted one of the best attacking line-ups in the division.

The mood around Anfield was distinctly gloomy as their title chase had been dealt a serious blow by the results as the Seasiders now climbed above them into second spot behind Bury. The pressure on the players was turned up a notch after this defeat because everything away from the field was dependent on the results on it. Crowds had been steadily building due to their recent string of impressive wins, but an early exit from the FA Cup before the lucrative First Round Proper had already set alarm bells ringing. The defeat to Northwich ruled out any chance of bagging a top side in the competition. This expensively assembled squad could well have been competing in the first division had Houlding got his way in the summer with the league application.

The board were working hard behind the scenes to organise high profile opposition for their friendly matches and the calibre of teams they could attract for these clearly showed the respect that they were commanding from other clubs around the country, but as it stood they were simply Turkish Delight—full of promise. Any more defeats and then the board would have to prepare for the unthinkable as they would be staring down the abyss of another season in the Lancashire League.

A week later Liverpool had to again make the trip to Blackpool, this time it was to face a mid-table South Shore side at Bloomfield Road on Christmas Eve which was the start of a busy holiday programme of games. The seaside resort was in its Victorian heyday and could easily support two sides, but South

Shore and Blackpool were to combine just five years later to form the side we know today as they both fell on harder times. South Shore were regarded as the best of the Fylde teams having completely revamped their team over the summer months including raiding Higher Walton and taking no less than five of their first team players to the coast. In W. Mather they had one of the sharpest shooters in the division and a striker coveted by every other team in the division. It was in defence that South Shore prided themselves. And they proved a tough nut to crack for McKenna's men as Tom Wylie hit the only goal of the game after five minutes to get them back to winning ways and keep them in touch with the leading pair.

Off the field there was trouble in the league as Liverpool Caledonians had finally been put into liquidation by their directors and their results expunged from the table. There had long been speculation about their future and whispers of financial irregularities at the club. Liverpool, like many other clubs, supplemented their league income by holding friendly matches which were essential to keep the club on a sound financial footing. This holiday period was the ideal time for such exhibition matches and in order to avoid the same fate as their neighbours the Liverpool board had agreed to host Sheffield United just 48 hours later on Boxing Day. Around 4,500 paid their money to watch a full strength side win by a single goal from Tom Wylie for the second game in a row. Hot on the heels of this game was the visit of Southport Central who made the short trip to put on a show for the fans the very next day where the two played out an entertaining 2–2 draw. The two games at Anfield provided good entertainment for the supporters and raised some welcome funds, but they also allowed the team to iron out any problems on the pitch and work on set pieces in a match environment. Nonetheless, they were still a side show as their fight for the league title was harder now than it was a week previously.

Liverpool ended the year by hosting fourth placed Heywood Central for the first time in the league on New Year's Eve. The game was one of the few to survive the weather. Both teams decided to go ahead with the match despite the fact that the ground was frozen solid and there were still a few inches of snow on the pitch, although the fans helped clear as much as they could before the game. The pair had played out a 1–1 draw in a friendly match at Central's Bamford Road ground only two weeks before in which John Miller was on target for Liverpool. Heywood had recovered from their terrible start to the season and had hit a rich vein of form in recent weeks which included a 5–1 Boxing Day demolition job away to leaders Bury. Liverpool, though, were in no mood to be overawed and had to put together a decent run of wins if they were to stay in touch with the leaders let alone put any real pressure on them. Further defeats would all but end their title dreams and as such McKenna made the bold move of dropping an off colour Smith because of his poor displays in recent games. McQue was brought back into midfield and the hugely versatile Matt McQueen, who had excelled as a half-back in recent weeks and even appeared at full-back on occasions, was pushed up front to take Smith's place amongst the forwards.

Liverpool: S Ross, goal; A Hannah and D McLean, full-backs; J McCartney, J McQue and J McBride, half-backs; T Wylie, M McQueen, J Miller, J Cameron and H McQueen, forwards.

Heywood Central: Sharples, goal; Pearson and Evan, full-backs; Woolfall, Scholes and Reagan, half-backs; Jones, McWhinnie, Horsfield, Allan and Webster, forwards.

It was a big call to play the younger McQueen as a forward, but one that was to pay dividends instantly with the utility player combining well with Wylie down the right wing from the first attack and his shot from the edge of the penalty area was just tipped over the bar. Wylie floated over the resulting corner which was headed in by Miller for a flying start to the game. During their recent draw the Liverpool selection committee had clearly seen something in the Heywood defence they could exploit and the physical presence of Matt McQueen gave them added edge in the final third. He wreaked havoc amongst the Heywood defence by never letting them settle on the ball and always put them under pressure when they tried to clear their lines.

The visitors seemed stunned by going a goal down after only five minutes and, like a rabbit caught in the headlights, they froze in their tracks as Liverpool ran rings around them. Literally in the case of Wylie and Matt McQueen to the absolute delight of the fans who were loudly cheering as the pair continued to put their markers on toast with their winding runs on a frozen pitch as a winter freeze was starting to take hold. The crowd at this match was down on previous gates as another favourite Victorian pastime was to take centre stage in the city in the form of a huge skating rink which proved to be a bigger distraction on the day.

Wylie was in inspired form for this game and was

Heywood's tormentor in chief as he drove his side forward in search of a second. And Wylie was to press home their advantage with two strikes in quick succession in his best game of the season so far. His first was a gem of a goal and the pick of the pair as he was sent racing clear of the defence by an inch perfect ball from McQue before sliding the ball home with a cool finish. The forward was attracting a lot of attention from fans around the country with his exploits in front of goal as his name seemed to be ever present on the score sheet. His growing reputation brought with it extra attention from the defenders and in this game he was subjected to some particularly nasty challenges from the Heywood players. But Wylie brushed off the painful tackles and got his revenge by showing his tormentors a clean pair of heels.

Credit to the Heywood lads in that they did not let their heads drop and got one back to make it 3–1 from the penalty spot, but any thoughts of a dramatic comeback by their fans were soon snuffed out as McLean scored twice to put the game beyond the visitors. They did, however, score a consolation goal for the fans to talk about on the way home from the penalty spot after a clumsy challenge by the otherwise dependable McLean, but Matt McQueen added a sixth after combining well with his brother to work an opening before applying the finish. The result put them back into second place just two points behind Bury and still with a game in hand on the leaders who had beaten Fleetwood 3–1 that afternoon.

Liverpool were to face Heywood again only days later in the second of three games away from Anfield. First up though, was a trip to mid-table

Fairfield on the Monday on a pitch that was by now bordering on dangerous. The ruts from the previous game had now frozen in place making the ground very difficult for a player to keep their feet. The Liverpool players adapted better to the conditions and they easily brushed aside Heywood 4-1 with goals from Cameron, Hugh McQueen, Miller and the prolific Wylie. The result was enjoyed all the more because Blackpool could only draw at home to this Fairfield side a couple of days earlier.

Beating Heywood again, though, would prove a much harder proposition and their task was made all the more difficult by the fact that the country was fully in the grip of a fierce winter and the game had to be played in snow that was six inches deep in places as the pitch had not and could not be cleared before kick-off. A howling wind was raging through the Bamford Road ground—many games up and down the country had to be called off and this was one of the few that survived the weather.

Out for revenge it was the visitors who started with the gale at their backs and had the best of the early exchanges. The home side started with the same side that was so soundly beaten only a week previously and they were determined not to allow a repeat. Ross, though, was equal to anything that the Heywood strikers could throw at him and pulled off a number of good saves in the opening few minutes in. He was beaten early on from a powerfully struck indirect free-kick, but it was ruled out as the ball did not touch a second player on the way onto the net by the referee. Lady Luck was clearly smiling on the Liverpool defence as Ross was again called upon to pull off a smart save in his line after the ball cannoned off the post and although the Central players were convinced it had crossed the line the referee, Mr Smalley of Blackburn, disagreed and the game remained goalless—just. The game was not all one-way traffic though, as Hugh McQueen and Wylie both hit shots narrowly over the bar and McQueen also had a free-kick headed off the line. There was no doubt that it was the home side who, aided in no small part by the hurricane strength wind, had the better of the play and it was only a matter of time before they took the lead when a free-kick was belted past Ross by Woolfall. The goal seemed to shake the visitors into action with McCartney being denied by a good save from Sharples and Miller shooting over from inside the box. Their revival was short lived as they were soon on the back foot as Central once again dominated the play and Liverpool did well keep the score at just 1–0 at half-time and looked forward to a change of ends as the elements would be in their favour.

The second half was a very different story as the now wind assisted Liverpool were very much on top. McLean was unlucky not to get an equaliser straight after the break when he whipped in a curling free-kick that was headed off the line by Evans. But it was only a matter of time before they did get on the scoreboard and it was Wylie who got them back on level terms in the second half with his 14th strike of the season. With the weather playing a huge part in the game the Liverpool players were encouraged to shoot on sight of goal as they went in search of a winner even though Central boasted an internationally capped goalkeeper in Sharples. McBride duly earned them both points with a curling effort from distance that flew over the head of the stranded goalkeeper and nestled in the back of the net. H. McQueen was in imperious form on the left wing and set up Wylie for a third late on with an inch perfect cross. But the former Everton man missed the target and a game spoiled as a spectacle in the main by the foul weather ended 2–1 to the visitors. Liverpool were now level at the top of the league with Bury on 22 points after stringing together a winning run of four games in a row. Both had identical records having each won 11 of their 13 games, but the Greater Manchester side had a superior goal difference having scored 61 goals while only letting in 16 compared to Liverpool who had 46 in the 'Goals For' column and 11 in the 'Goals Against'.

Lancashire League up to 7 January 1893

	Pld	W	L	D	F	A	Pts
Bury	13	11	2	0	51	16	22
LIVERPOOL	13	11	2	0	46	11	22
Blackpool	11	9	1	1	40	14	19
Fleetwood Rangers	12	5	6	1	25	55	11
Heywood Central	10	5	5	0	26	27	10
Rossendale	10	4	4	2	28	23	10
West Manchester	11	4	5	2	33	33	10
Fairfield	13	2	5	6	20	30	9
South Shore	10	2	3	5	28	28	9
Higher Walton	10	3	11	1	20	75	7
Southport Central	11	3	8	0	15	20	6
Nelson	11	2	8	1	27	44	5

7

NEW YEAR BRINGS NEW HOPE

In mid-January Liverpool made their second trip to West Manchester as the race for the championship was shaping into a three way fight between McKenna's men, Blackpool and Bury. Liverpool may have already secured back-to-back wins against West Manchester back in October where they came out 3–1 victors firstly at home in the league and by the same score during the first away tie when they met in the Lancashire Cup a week later and although they were now languishing in mid-table due to inconsistent results they remained, nonetheless, the only club to have beaten high-flying Blackpool in the league so far in the season.

The return to West Manchester was more of a sombre affair than the last visit as the club was mourning the sudden death of one of its directors, Mr A. Kershaw, at the age of just 33 and who left a wife and three children. The Liverpool lads steeled themselves to face a team with something extra to play for and so it proved as the game was one of the hardest fought of the campaign so far. The game kicked off with all flags at the club being flown at half mast as a sign of respect and with the West Manchester players refusing to give an inch, it was no real surprise that the match degenerated into a tough slog played out in the midfield. Neither goalkeeper had much to do throughout the game as the ball rarely left the middle third of the pitch as the scrappy game finished goalless after 90 minutes. Miller and Hugh McQueen had a couple of half chances, but that was as good as it got for the visitors really as they were unable to capitalise on the fact that West Manchester were without their first choice goalkeeper through injury and played their veteran full-back Frank Sugg between the sticks. The home fans were the happier of the two sets of supporters as their side had slightly the better of the play, but, on the whole, a share of the points was a fair reward for both their day's work and it spoke volumes that Duncan McLean was easily the man of the match. Although it did mean that Liverpool were no longer joint leaders of the division.

A week later was a trip to Bury for a top of the table clash. The league refused to sanction the match, but as the fixture had been agreed between the clubs they decided to go ahead with the game on a friendly basis and take a share of the gate receipts. Both sides took the opportunity to rest players and this was reflected in a lower than otherwise expected gate. Nonetheless it would give both sides the chance to get the measure of each other psychologically for the crunch league fixture in two weeks' time. Bury were perhaps the most annoyed by the actions of the league as they came into the game on the back of a nine goal thrashing of Higher Walton. Liverpool decided to give both Hannah and Hugh McQueen the day off while Bury rested two of their key men in Warburton and Jobson and were denied the chance to play the excellent forward Wilkinson because of an injury to his leg that prevented him from taking part. The fans who did show up were treated to an excellent exhibition match that flowed from end to end as their two contrasting styles made for an intriguing encounter. With their huge Scottish contingent, Liverpool were masters of the controlled passing game whereas Bury preferred the more direct style of play that prevailed in England at the time. Matt McQueen dropped back into defence to replace Hannah while Kelvin operated down the left flank as the outside forward.

Liverpool won the toss and played with the wind to their backs in the first half. The two teams produced a tight affair that one goal either way would have settled as a contest. Right from the start the match took on a cup-tie feel as this was a one-off match and flowed entertainingly. The visitors were full of the tricks and flicks that their fans had come to expect from such an accomplished, patient and stylish side whereas Bury were more efficient and direct in their approach, but were no less entertaining for their eagerness to get into the Liverpool half and have a go at goal from the earliest moment. McVean thought he had ended the deadlock just before half-time when he broke clear of the defence and slid the ball neatly past the advancing Lowe in the Bury goal and into the net only for his cool finish to be ruled out as he was yards offside and so honours were even at the interval.

When the game resumed Bury now had the wind in their favour and were quick to use it to their advantage with a long ball over the top that wrong-footed the Liverpool defence and McLean did well to win a foot-race with Barlow to clear with a superbly timed sliding challenge on the pacey forward. The game continued in much the same way for the rest of the half with both sides creating chances to score. Both Kelso and McVean should have bagged goals for Liverpool while McLean was in imperious form at the back to deny the lively Bury lads from sneaking the winner. The two best chances of the match came in the dying minutes. First, with less than five minutes left on the clock, McLean broke down another Bury attack and sent Wylie scampering away with the ball in his own half. The former Everton man ended a bustling run at the edge of the Bury box with a thunderbolt of a shot that Lowe tipped round the post with his finger tips to loud applause from both sets of fans. The home side cleared the resulting corner and set about stealing the glory for themselves and for once Ross was beaten by a curling shot from Plant only for his effort to cannon back off the post as the referee blew his whistle and so it was that the enjoyable game at Gigg Lane finished goalless.

For their last game in January, Liverpool returned to the Lancashire Cup and hosted second division side Darwin in front of a bumper crowd, swelled no doubt by the fact that both Everton and Bootle were playing away that weekend. With Liverpool not having played at home for almost an entire month the pitch was in perfect condition for two passing sides to ply their trade. The Liverpool fans and players alike were eager to test themselves against league opposition in this cup competition as they had one eye on promotion and this would provide them with a yard stick to measure themselves against. Injuries were now taking their toll on the club and McKenna had to wait for the results of a number of fitness tests before deciding on the team. Andrew

Hannah passed his, just, but Sydney Ross did not. They lined up as follows:

Liverpool: B McOwen, goal; A Hannah and D McLean, full-backs; J McCartney, J McQue and M McQueen, half-backs; T Wylie, J Smith, J Miller, M McVean and H McQueen, forwards.

Darwen: Kenyon, goal; Leach and Orr, full-backs; Fish, Maxwell and McEvoy, half-backs; Wade, Campbell, McKennie, Entwistle and Sutherland, forwards.

The visitors kicked off in front of the 8,000 fans packed into the ground and applied early pressure to the Liverpool goal. Duncan McLean put in a couple of strong challenges early and soon it was McKenna's men who had a chance to show the league boys what they were made of. An excellent shot from Miller earned them an early corner and allowed Liverpool to get off to the perfect start. Matt McQueen drifted in an inch perfect corner from the right that McVean jumped well to head home after only eight minutes on the clock. The fans were delirious and produced a deafening noise within the ground. The visitors were clearly rattled and Hugh McQueen was causing havoc down the left wing. Twice Liverpool came close to doubling their lead, but the score remained 1–0 after 15 minutes as the visitors began to compose themselves. The early goal proved to be crucial as afterwards Darwen shaped up to be a very good side as they set about getting back on level terms.

McLean, despite showing good promise in the opening minutes, for once looked shaky at the back as he struggled to cope with the intelligent play from the Darwen forwards. Sutherland and Entwistle were the pick of the visiting attack, but McOwen, with the help of Matt McQueen restricted them to a couple of corners just as they got into decent shooting positions. Liverpool were equal to everything that was thrown at them and were unlucky not to get more goals as they hit their second wind with 10 minutes left in the first period. Miller and Smith exchanged passes in the midfield with some style and the latter set up Wylie on the edge of the box with a deft pass but in rounding the last defender the striker left himself a tight angle to shoot from and his shot was pushed around the near post by the Kenyon in the Darwen goal. The 'keeper did even better on the resulting corner by fisting the ball a good 30 yards to clear their lines.

Wylie had another couple of chances to bag a second goal before the break and turned provider as the half wore on when he returned the compliment to Smith by cutting the ball back from the by-line for Smith, who, despite the lack of a 'Mac' in his surname, was in fact Scottish. The versatile Ayrshire born player was one of the pioneers of football in the north east having played for Newcastle East End (who eventually went on to form Newcastle United) before moving to and eventually featuring in every position for Sunderland where he won the title before moving to Liverpool in the summer of 1892. A popular player in his time on Tyneside he left Liverpool for The Wednesday at the end of the season before returning to the north east where he featured for a further two seasons, eventually retiring from football in 1896 when 'Jock' Smith, as he was affectionately known locally, became a licensee in Byker. He died after a short illness in 1911, but such was the affection and respect he was held in by both sets of fans that many turned up for the benefit match in aid of his widow at St James' Park.

His undoubted skill left him for that brief second in front of goal as he missed the target from close range with the goal begging. The mark of a good player can be measured by many things, but one of the most important is how they respond to failure and Smith showed the class that won him a championship medal at Sunderland as he refused to let his head drop and continued to look dangerous. First, he danced his way through the defence just minutes later to work himself a yard of space to shoot only to be denied by an excellent tackle from McAvoy just as he was about to let fly with a shot and then drew an excellent save from Kenyon in the next attack as Liverpool were running riot against the league side in a thrilling end to the half. Darwen mounted the occasional counter-attack which caused concern as the game became more open, but Liverpool ended the half the stronger.

During the respite the players will have had it impressed upon them how important a second goal would be if they were to get some clear blue water between themselves and Darwen and Wylie was inches away from getting it after the re-start. The forward showed a neat piece of skill to fashion a gap to shoot through but his shot was curled just wide of the post. Both sides continued to play their part in an exciting game with Darwen looking the more threatening of the pair the longer the match went on and there was more than one heart stopping moment for the Anfield crowd. Soon after the break Darwen had a corner which fell to McKennie on the edge of the box and he struck the ball through the crowd with some ferocity. McOwen looked to be at least a yard over the line when he made the save, but the goal was not given and both sets of players carried on.

Midway through the second half McOwen, playing his one and only game for the club that season, was eventually beaten by a terrific curling shot from outside the box, but the relief was felt by all when the ball hit the post and bounced clear. The popular goalkeeper was to feature more heavily for the club in the future, but with Ross in such great form he found his chances limited. The talented keeper had the honour of becoming the youngest goalkeeper in the league when he turned out for his local side Blackburn at the age of just 15. This is all the more remarkable when you consider the punishment that was dished out to goalkeepers at the time. They were given little or no protection from the referees and were often bundled into the net with a well placed shoulder barge. In these days it was normal practice for a player to 'take care of the goalkeeper' in that it was a much more physical game than today and barging or body checking an opponent was not only legal, but also actively encouraged because the crowd loved to see a bit of argy-bargy. The physical side of the game was a feature until the latter half of the last century.

Film footage exists of the late, and truly great, Sir Nat Lofthouse, 'the Lion of Vienna', bundling Harry Gregg, a survivor of the Munich crash only months earlier, into the net during the 1958 FA Cup final under a high ball by a shoulder charge from the famous footballing knight. The goals stood and Bolton, the only club he ever played for, won 2–0. Lofthouse, who went on to score an amazing 30 goals in 33 appearances for England and earned his nickname for being knocked out while scoring the winner against Austria only to return after a couple of minutes off the pitch following a dose of smelling salts and a shrug of the shoulders. He said of the incident in his inimitable sanguine manner that 'in my day, there were plenty of fellas who would kick your bollocks off. The difference was that at the end of the match they would shake your hand and help you look for them!' Like many goalkeepers of his day, McOwen was not just tough, but also a cunning player who started the highly amusing practice of jumping up and pulling on the crossbar when the ball looked likely to hit it or sneak just under the woodwork so that the ball would sail harmlessly over the top.

The trick was very popular with fans as they thought it hilarious, but the FA took a very different view. In a bid to stop this, they ruled that a referee was allowed to award a goal if they thought that his actions had stopped one being scored. McOwen played well in this game as Liverpool rode their luck at times, but they were not outplayed. In fact, as in the first half, they ended strongly and could have snatched another goal.

The Darwen players faded towards the end as Liverpool produced some neat possession play to frustrate and tire their opponents. Smith and Miller continued to fluff their lines and on another day would have scored plenty after some excellent approach play from Hugh McQueen and McVean while Matt McQueen earned his money twice over behind them with a terrific performance. Liverpool held on to their lead until the final whistle and ran out slightly more comfortable winners than the 1–0 score-line suggests. With just a couple of jitters, particularly when the woodwork came to their rescue (without the assistance of McOwen's body weight), Liverpool held on and were rewarded with a mouth-watering semi-final tie against Bootle to be played over two legs in March.

With their cup campaign going well it was back to the league and a return to Gigg Lane to face the early pace setters, Bury. The importance of the task ahead for both sides could not be underestimated and the game was billed as the championship decider with the winner all-but sealing the title, and with that in mind there was not a spare seat in the ground and the fans flocked to see this epic encounter between the top two clubs in the division. Bury's slip up against Southport a couple of weeks earlier narrowed the gap between the two at the top and cranked up the pressure on the defending champions with Blackpool flying high also. Liverpool had so far exceeded all expectations, but the long season was starting to take its toll on their small squad of players. They lined up without Hugh McQueen as he had suffered a dead leg in their friendly match against Stoke at the beginning of the month and lost his battle to be fit for this important game. Liverpool started the game with Ross back in goal. Hannah was forced to play through the pain barrier as he had suffered a broken toe. This was not enough to keep the man of iron down and he joined McLean at the back. The half-backs for the match were McCartney, McQue and McBride. Wylie and Smith were to combine down the right and McVean and McQueen were on the opposite wing supplying the ammunition for Miller to fire.

In contrast, Bury had prepared well for the match by spending the week in a special training camp in Lancaster and were in good shape for the game and welcomed back the imposing figure of Warburton at the back and the versatile Jobson in midfield. The biggest cheer from the home fans was reserved for their talented forward Bourn who had been sidelined for three weeks as he trotted out onto the pitch.

A full line-up was as follows: Bury: Lowe, goal; Holt and Warburton, full-backs; Clegg, Jobson and G Ross, half-backs; Wilkinson, Spence, Barbour, Bourn and Plant, forwards.

Liverpool: S Ross, goal; A Hannah and D McLean, full-backs; J McCartney, M McBride, and J McQue, half-backs; T Wylie, J Smith, J Miller, M McVean and M McQueen, forwards.

A defeat for Bury would all but end their title hopes and because of this they set about Liverpool from the whistle in front of a full house of around 8,000 noisy fans. They were denied by a brilliant display at the back from McLean which drew equal measures of admiration and irritation from the Bury fans while his partner struggled with his injury. The defender continued to break down attack after attack as the home side took an early stranglehold on the game. Ross also played his part in goal with a string of fine saves from Wilkinson and Plant.

Liverpool managed only a couple of meaningful attempts at goal with Matt McQueen hitting the far post from a corner as the cross wind took the ball away from a lurking Smith. But they were eventually undone midway through the first half when the home side headed the opener after 22 minutes through Barbour. The forward was picked out perfectly from a corner by Plant as he dashed in from the right hand side of the box to ghost past Hannah to meet the curling cross from the left with his forehead. It was no less than they deserved for their creative play and sustained pressure. Barbour could have had a second just a few minutes later when he tried to lob the ball over Ross only for his effort to land on top of the net while Bourn drew two excellent saves from Ross as the half went on. The pressure from the home side was relentless, but Liverpool fought bravely against the onslaught and managed to keep the deficit down to just the one goal at the break giving them time to regroup over a cup of tea and came out for the second half with renewed vigour. Such was the comprehensive nature of the display from the home side that they earned a whopping nine corners in the first half to just one from Liverpool with the goal coming from the sixth delivery. But Bury were determined to carry on from where they left off after the break and the wind was soon knocked out of Liverpool's sails as this match report from the excellent *Athletic News* of 13 February 1893 recalls:

It speaks volumes for the character of the Liverpool defence that they only had one goal recorded against them at the interval, for two thirds of the warfare was carried on in their territory. Now that the visitors had the aid of a stiffish breeze, and only one point to rub off, their admirers were very hopeful as to the result. But a rude awakening was in store for them. The Gigg Lane men never slackened in their pace for a single moment and literally forced corners by the half dozen . . . sometimes three corners would be taken in rapid succession, and I may safely say that I have never in all my life seen corners better put in than they were by Wilkinson and Plant. In no single case was the ball sent behind, and the auburn-tinted cranium of McLean was ever to the fore in heading from under the bar, whilst Ross's keeping was of the A-1 brand. Lowe at the other end, had rarely anything to do, and more rarely still was he sorely pressed. Spence and Plant added goals for Bury, each success being the signal for a volley of cheers, and when time had expired Liverpool were beaten by three goals to nothing. As they won the first engagement at Anfield by four goals to nothing, they had thus a goal the better of their opponents on the season's doings. Bury are indeed champions on their own enclosure, and I can well understand that their friends declare there is no team like them. The dash and go of the forwards is like a wave of the sea dashing on the rocks, and it was this element that broke the visitors' defence. Once on the move, the ball seemed bound to finish up somewhere near the desired haven, and the unanimity between the whole of the forwards was ever noticeable—Wilkinson and Plant, for their dashing runs and smart centres, Spence and Bourn for their tasty passing, and Barbour for his unselfishness and excellent shooting came in for repeated commendation, each and all being vastly superior to the Liverpool front rank. The half-back division stuck to their work with great pluck, George Ross and Jobson continually shining, whilst Clegg was rarely at fault. Warburton and Holt left Lowe with little to do, and the little he did with perfect satisfaction. I expected better things of the visitors, particularly the front row. Several of them exhibited excellent command over the ball, and Smith and Wylie put in some telling runs, but every one of them lacked finish. Their powder was of a poor quality, and when they did let fly their shots never hurt anybody. McBride had a handful in the home right wing, but was not always second best, and I thought him cleverer than either of his colleagues. McLean did almost twice as much work as Hannah who was hampered by a bad toe, which accounted for his uneven kicking. Ross could certainly have gone back to Liverpool conscious of having done his duty fearlessly and effectively. No man could have kept goal better.

The defeat must have been a crushing blow to the spirits of Liverpool as they could see the title slipping away from them. The pain was from not so much the result as the manner in which it was delivered. Bury never gave them a chance to settle into their fluid passing game, indeed McKenna looked on as his side were hustled out of the match. Ross alone made five brilliant saves that he had no right to make and it was agreed that he was the man of the match by all who attended the game such was the mastery of his performance. At the end of the game the win was so complete that the fans of both teams applauded the victorious Bury side who were deserved winners. McLean shone at the back and, like Ross, could not be faulted despite the score-line. Without McLean the rampant Bury forwards would surely have scored far more than they did. With Blackpool running out 6–3 winners against mid-table Fairfield the result threw the championship race wide open again and Liverpool knew if they were to salvage anything from this season they could afford no more slip-ups in the league and hope that others around them would carelessly drop points.

Things were tight at the top of the table and despite the defeat, Liverpool were still in second place and they could move to within a point of Bury on 26 if they were to win their game in hand, but Bury's far superior goal difference was akin to having an extra point. Blackpool were also still lurking in third place on 21 points, but despite their lack of points they had an ace of their own up their sleeve with having three games in hand on the leaders and two on Liverpool on 23 points. Liverpool had to pick themselves up and cobble together a nice little run of wins so the trip across Lancashire to rock bottom

Nelson could not have arrived at a better time. What they needed was a confidence boosting victory and two points in the bag if they were to get their title challenge back on track. And with just two wins to their name all season, Nelson could be the team to provide them with a much needed fillip.

Liverpool kicked off and set about their lowly opposition like any hungry beast would its prey on a sticky and heavy pitch. Soon after kick-off Hugh McQueen combined well with McVean to carve himself an excellent opening but his audacious effort was just a touch too high and landed on the roof of the net. Liverpool continued to miss chance after chance as they had by far the lion's share of the chances and it was starting to look as if it was going to be a frustrating day until McVean finally broke the deadlock. He ended a winding run by thumping the ball into the net after 20 minutes. The goal seemed to settle their nerves and Miller added a second on the half hour to send Liverpool in to enjoy their half-time refreshment two goals to the good.

Unusually, Liverpool looked lacklustre after the break and paid for taking their foot off the pedal by conceding two quick goals to make the game all square as Nelson, who had clearly not been reading the script, threw the form book out the window and threatened to end Liverpool's chase for the title there and then. McKenna's side had to dig deep and, to their immense credit, they played their way back into the game. A win was vital if they were to keep the pressure on at the top of the table. They may have left it late, but Miller proved to be the man of the hour as he scored a screamer to give Liverpool the win with just five minutes left to play and keep their season alive. This was not the pushover they expected, but it was a vital win with Bury having beaten Fairfield 3–0 and Blackpool earned their two points with a 3–1 win over fourth placed Heywood Central so it remained 'as you were' at the summit.

Next up was a home game against third from bottom Southport Central. Despite their lowly position the visitors had one of the better defensive records in the division. Their problem all season had been scoring goals and no one else had found the back of the opposition net fewer times than the Southport team. That said, the visitors almost had the perfect start when Kenny Davenport sent a free-kick whistling just past the post from 20 yards out. Liverpool soon got into their groove with McBride putting their noses in front after quarter of an hour when he linked up well with both Hugh McQueen and McVean before smashing the ball past the outstretched Southport goalkeeper, Jim Gee, and into the net. The goal whetted the appetite of the Liverpool strikers and now, with their tails up, they pushed hard for another.

McBride again was at the end of some excellent play with the ball being threaded through the Central midfield and into the box where the former Renton man hit another of his thunderous drives. This time, though, Gee was able, not only to reach the ball, but also to hold onto it at the second attempt as the pair of them collided while battling to be first to the rebound. Both were roundly cheered for their fighting spirit as they clambered to their feet to continue with the game. It was not unusual for a goalkeeper to have to climb out from under two or three bodies in these games as the forwards tried everything to either release the ball from the grasp or smash them over the line with a bone juddering shoulder barge. The ball remained in the Central half for the majority of the 45 with Liverpool trying to turn their superiority of possession and territory into goals. Both McVean and Hugh McQueen had decent efforts saved as Gee kept his side in the game. With half-time approaching Joe McQue lined up a free-kick from a dangerous position just outside the box. The former Celtic man took his time before unleashing a rasping drive that flew through the crowded area and skimmed the bar as it flew over with Gee standing no chance of reaching the ball, and even less chance of stopping it even if he had.

Matt McQueen, who had already twice fired shots narrowly over the bar, finally found his range and made it 2–0 with a clinical strike with 10 minutes to go in the first half. The second goal seemed to shake Southport out of their slumber and they started to offer a little more in attack, but it was nowhere near enough to trouble Hannah who twice snuffed out promising breaks in their infancy with his superb positioning which allowed him to be in the right place at the vital time to frustrate the Central attackers and delight the home crowd who were mightily impressed by how simple he made it look. The fans felt unlucky they did not see their team put in a third on the stroke of half-time when Gee pulled off yet another great save. This time it was from Wylie who cut in from the right and tried to curl the ball over the 'keeper and into the top corner only for Gee to palm the ball away while back-pedalling furiously. Hugh McQueen was first to the rebound, but again Gee was able to clear his lines even though he was under a lot pressure from the now rampant Liverpool forwards.

Central fared better after the break when W. Hastings was sent clear of the defence for the first time with a perfectly timed run only to be denied as Ross flew off his line to clear the danger. They matched Liverpool in midfield for the rest of the game and neither side now fashioned much in the way of chances and it proved to be a comfortable day's work for Liverpool as Southport offered little more in the way of attacking and could still be playing today and not have scored. The only downside for Liverpool was they did not score more goals against a below par side and improve their goal difference. Liverpool had, without doubt, some of the best strikers in the division in Smith and Miller but the forwards all failed to convert some good opportunities into goals.

They were not the only ones guilty of not making the most out of a good opportunity as McQue rattled the bar with a ferocious effort from midfield after opting for power instead of precision when a cool head would have served him better. Gee did impress in goal, but that could not excuse the lamentable performance from all concerned in front of goal. Bury didn't have a fixture this weekend so the win left Liverpool just one point off the pace with the same number of games played. Dangerously, Blackpool beat their local rivals South Shore 4–0 to keep them in the hunt with a pair of games in hand.

The turn of March brought the visit of lowly Nelson to Anfield as the pair clashed for the second time in a matter of weeks. This was always going to be a tough game for the visitors despite their excellent effort in the narrow defeat in mid-February and their worst fears were realised within five minutes when Matt McQueen scored the opener.

The younger of the two McQueen brothers, Matt, was proving to be one of the best signings of the new side because of his versatility and his goals. Matt was to go down in the folklore of Liverpool football club as one of its greatest ever servants. During his time at the club he went on to play in every position including as a regular replacement for McOwen in goal over the next few seasons and even won two second division championship medals playing both in goal and outfield positions during the season. Even when he retired he continued to give plenty back to the sport he loved by becoming a referee before being welcomed onto the board as a director of the club with open arms in 1919. A five year spell as manager of the club was to follow in 1923 despite having lost his leg in a traffic accident and he won a first division winner's medal as manager in 1923. McQueen never left Liverpool after moving to Kemlyn Road in the 1890s and staying there until his death in 1944.

It was his scrambled effort that got the breakthrough against struggling Nelson whose players must have felt it was going to be a long afternoon as they had not only a rampant Liverpool side to deal with but also the wind, the sun and the partisan crowd against them. The home side piled on the pressure and all the forwards missed chances to increase the lead in the first half as it was all hands to the pumps in the Nelson defence as they hung on until half-time having rarely ventured out of their own half. McCartney was disappointed not to be on the score sheet just before the break when his long, dipping drive was tipped over the bar by the goalkeeper as there was no one in the box to stop him reaching the ball.

Wylie was having a strange off day and was guilty of missing the best of the chances when clean through on goal. Liverpool had their lead, but following the way Nelson fought back in the last encounter to overturn a two goal lead they will not have felt at ease with the score-line. The home side had enough of the ball to fashion another goal, but their only reward was a substantial number of corners which they could not convert. No doubt concerns about this will have been raised by the pragmatic McKenna in his talk to the players during the short break. The lack of goals from his team despite overwhelming superiority was becoming a familiar tale in recent weeks and could spell disaster for his charges if they were to drop points by losing or drawing a game they should have won at a canter.

The second half brought about much of the same and it must have looked like a training session of attack against the defence as again Liverpool never let their opposition out of their half. M. McQueen got his, and Liverpool's, second of the game with a simply brilliant solo effort. After dancing his way through the Nelson defence he drilled the ball into the net with a fearsome drive that left the keeper with no chance with just five minutes having elapsed since the re-start. Minutes later he got on the end of a Wylie corner but the woodwork stood between him and a deserved hat-trick. The visitors played much better in the second half, but things only got worse for them as Liverpool bagged the third and final goal of the game when Hugh McQueen smacked in a free-kick as they soundly beat rock bottom Nelson 3–0. While the Blackpool players rested, Bury stayed top of the table as they left Heywood with two points following an astonishing

10–1 demolition of Central in front of 6,000 fans to increase their already impressive goal haul. The home side felt they were hard done by because the opening goal from Barbour had in fact missed the target and tore through the side netting. The event must have played on the minds of the players and in some way goes to explaining the rout. But it could not hide the fact that Bury were keeping up the pressure on their rivals at a crucial time of the season as there was now only four games left to decide who was to be crowned the champions of Lancashire and have the chance to appear in the football league next season.

Lancashire League up to 4 March 1893

	Pld	W	L	D	F	A	Pts
Bury	18	15	3	0	71	19	30
LIVERPOOL	18	14	3	1	54	16	29
Blackpool	15	12	2	1	53	21	25
West Manchester	17	8	5	4	55	40	20
Heywood Central	16	9	7	0	44	46	19
Rossendale	17	8	7	2	43	40	18
Fleetwood Rangers	16	6	7	3	33	44	15
South Shore	16	4	7	5	39	49	13
Fairfield	18	4	9	5	30	44	13
Southport Central	18	5	13	0	25	39	10
Higher Walton	19	3	14	2	27	99	8
Nelson	18	3	14	1	47	64	7

8

SETTLING OLD SCORES

The Liverpool players had a chance to take their mind off the pressures of final stages of the league campaign with a return to their Lancashire Cup campaign and a much anticipated tie at Bootle who, while no longer the force on Merseyside that they were only a couple of years ago, still presented a difficult challenge. The second round game would have the added edge of the well established Bootle team getting the chance to put down the young upstarts of Liverpool for the bragging rights in the city that weekend and would also settle the arguments about who could claim to be the second team in the city, if you were to accept that Everton were still occupying first place, as the two teams had never met before after their pre-season friendly was called off months earlier.

There is no doubting the fact that Bootle were the bigger club at the time as they were founder members of the Football Alliance in 1889. The alliance merged with the football league a year before and Bootle had the honour of becoming founder members of the inaugural Second division. This team reached the quarter finals of the FA Cup in 1890 only to lose to the eventual winners, Blackburn Rovers. Such was the excitement surrounding the tie that the biggest crowd of the season by some distance packed into their Hawthorne Road home for kick-off. The Bootle board for their part had made sure the ground was in perfect condition for this showpiece game with so much at stake. They were no doubt still aggrieved that they missed out on a place in the inaugural league to the former Anfield side some years before.

The fact that many within the city still bore ill-will towards Houlding and his team since the great split last summer added more spice to this already potentially explosive encounter. And there is no doubt that the ranks of the Bootle fans were swelled by those who supported Everton so they could vent their spleen at Houlding. Bootle had been on the decline for some years and the last time their ground was packed so full was three years ago to the day when they drew against Everton. McKenna will have warned his players that they would have to play to the occasion and the crowd as well as the opposition if they were to get through this derby match.

The teams lined up as follows: Bootle: McLoughlan, goal; Hutchinson and Arridge, full-backs; Robertson, Hughes and McEwan, half-backs; Clarkin, Gallocher, Grierson, Branson and Montgomery, forwards.

Liverpool: Ross, goal; Hannah and McLean, full-backs; McCartney, McQue and McBride, half-backs; Wylie, M McQueen, Miller, McVean and H McQueen, forwards.

Both sides came into the game on the back of some decent results and there was a huge roar to greet Grierson as he kicked off into the brilliant sunshine, but McQue set the tone of the match immediately by robbing the ball in midfield and

Liverpool were straight onto the attack with Hugh McQueen finishing a slick move with a fearsome drive from the edge of the box but McLoughlan was able to get his hands to it. The game was now flowing from end-to-end and despite the early promise Liverpool found themselves a goal down after just five minutes. Bootle caught them with a classic sucker-punch on the counter-attack as they probed them looking for a weakness in their defence. Montgomery was the architect as he worked himself a bit of space by the touchline before releasing Clarkin with an inch perfect through ball that had the fans purring and the striker slid the ball past Ross with a clinical finish.

They could have been two down just minutes later as the pair combined again, but this time Clarkin could not keep his shot on target. This was not the start that Liverpool were hoping for and now they had a huge task ahead of them. By half-time the pattern of the game was set. Liverpool had the wind and the sun in their favour after the break and continued to play the better football and created chances. Liverpool thought they had drawn level when H. McQueen headed home from a corner, but the referee waved away their claims that McLoughlan was over the line when he caught the ball and so had little to show for all their patient play as the Bootle defence stood firm with the threat of getting caught on the break by the league side a constant one.

It was apparent to all that Liverpool would have to do something special after the interval if they were to get back on level terms. But disaster was to befall McKenna's men in the second half as Bootle launched an attack down their left wing and Ross, who saw the danger early, flew out of his goal to save at the winger's feet, but in doing so received a sickening blow to the head which knocked him out and the ball loose. Bootle's centre forward, Gallocher, ever the poacher, added insult to the injury by turning the ball into the net for Bootle's second goal of the game. The Liverpool players were furious with the referee for awarding the goal and made their protests known to the official, but with little success and Liverpool now had a mountain to climb. Ross was stretchered off and taken to hospital with concussion and Liverpool now found themselves two goals and a man down with just minutes left in the cup tie. They redoubled their efforts and, with Matt McQueen taking over between the sticks, got one back through his brother following some good work from Miller in the build up, but it was not enough as 'Brutal' Bootle ran out 2–1 winners in this fiercely contested cup tie with Gallocher almost adding a third in the dying moments of the encounter but he fired his effort just inches over the bar.

The disappointment of getting dumped out of the cup was overshadowed by the injury to Ross. The blow he took to the head was indeed a serious one and he was not released from Stanley hospital for a week such was the perilous state of his health. His heroics in the Liverpool goal were one of the cornerstones upon which the mean Liverpool defence was built. An essential stop for McKenna on his recruitment drive in the previous summer was Cambuslang, a tough mining region of Glasgow some six miles south-east of the city centre, to cast his eye on a goalkeeper who had been earning rave reviews in Ross. The team were formed in 1874, but like many of the early sides went into liquidation just 23 years later as they were the unexpected victims of professionalism. Their time may have been only short but they were one of the 11 founding members of the Scottish football league in 1890 and were a force to be reckoned with in their brief existence. They won the Lanarkshire Association Cup in 1884 and 1885, but their most notable achievement was being the runners-up of the Scottish Cup in 1888, having soundly thrashed Abercorn 10–1 in the semi-finals. They also won the first ever Glasgow Cup that year too. In Ross's last year with the club they finished a respectable fourth having thumped a much fancied Renton side 8–2 in their opening fixture but the following season they finished poorly and dropped out of the league having finished one place off the bottom and joined the rival Football Alliance instead only to be wound up in 1897.

The club considered themselves lucky to have signed him, such was the reputation he had built north of the border with Clydesdale. In one match his side were thumped 5–0 by Celtic, but he claimed the man of the match award such was the calibre of his play. It was noted at the time that Celtic would have won by a cricket score if it were not for him. The performances made him very popular with the fans who gave him the nickname of 'McRoss' in a bid to not let him feel left out of the 'Team of all the Macs'. Ross was never to play football again as another blow to the head like that would surely have ended his life. He returned to Scotland with his wife Mary where they had four children and went to work in the shipyards as a tinsmith and gasfitter to support his young family.

The loss of Ross was compounded as McOwen, his

replacement, was having trouble getting the time off from his job as a dentist to feature in the team. McOwen was so successful in his chosen trade that he retired from professional football a year later despite having an excellent season for them in their second year because he could make far more money away from the sport and eventually played out his career as an amateur for Blackpool. Matt McQueen stepped forward and was chosen to carry on as a stand-in between the sticks following his impressive debut against Bootle. This was a position he was to keep for the rest of the season as the versatile player impressed all at the club with his performances. In an odd twist of fate the cup was to return to Anfield within weeks as the Lancashire FA chose Liverpool's impressive ground as the venue for the following semi-final between Bootle and Preston North End which the latter won by an astonishing six goals to four.

Liverpool had once again to show their powers of recovery and put the thoroughly disappointing defeat behind them as they entertained mid-table Fairfield who had just beaten West Manchester 3–1. With all eyes on how the new goalkeeper would cope in the game there must have been extra pressure on the full-backs to put in an excellent performance and protect McQueen. And the defenders did not let their manager down, moreover Duncan McLean opened the scoring with his first league goal of the season producing a magnificent free-kick as Liverpool took their frustration out on their opponents. Miller hit two more before the break as Liverpool put Fairfield to the sword as he linked up well with his young strike partner, Phillip Kelly, who had impressed on his debut against Rossendale. It didn't get any better for the hapless visitors after the break as Wylie well and truly put the game beyond them when he rounded off a slick passing move from midfield by curling in the fourth of the match before Hugh McQueen wrapped up the win with a well taken fifth with his head.

The win was significant in that it put Liverpool on top of the table with Bury not featuring in the league that weekend. The greater Manchester side did not play the weekend after as Liverpool were again at home, this time they hosted the return match against South Shore on a warm Spring afternoon. Andrew Hannah lost the toss and so Liverpool were forced to kick-off against the elements.

With just five minutes gone Liverpool showed their class with a well worked opening goal. Miller and the returning Smith, who had not played since the last time these two teams clashed on Christmas Eve, combined well to set Wylie clear of the defence and the winger greedily tucked the ball away.

South Shore were a better team than their position suggested and fought back from the kick-off, but as ever McQue was quick to pounce on any danger and broke up any attacks as quickly as they started. What made McQue a class apart from all the other ball players around at that time was what he did with the ball after winning it. The midfielder had an excellent eye for a pass and could turn defence into attack with devastating effect. On this occasion he sent Hugh McQueen down the wing and the flying Scotsman cut in from the left with the South Shore defenders in his wake and drilled his shot towards the far corner which the South Shore goalkeeper did well to push away. But it was just a taste of what was to come as Liverpool continued to dominate and soon added a second when Hugh

McQueen ended a bustling run with a cross into the box that the South Shore defenders failed to clear and McVean managed to flick into the goal with a cheeky back-heel. While the crowd loved the audacity of McVean's goal they were left in open-mouthed awe at what was to follow. The visitors attacked in a bid to claw their way back into this game but McBride broke down the move by robbing Parkinson just as he was about to pull the trigger and sent Hugh McQueen away down the left with the ball. His cross into the box was smashed into the net spectacularly by Miller with an overhead kick. From defending their own box Liverpool had stylishly scored a third in a matter of seconds and wrapped up the game. It was no more than they deserved for their first half dominance and they silenced any who thought the pressure of a title chase would make them more conservative and timid in their play.

South Shore pulled one back when they hit a purple patch after the break, but it only seemed to inspire Liverpool to play better and Miller scored twice more, albeit one was ruled out by the referee, as Liverpool swept South Shore aside with a deserved 4–1 win. It could have been argued that the side were not playing at their best because of matters off the field. Talks were well under way about their merger with their seaside rivals Blackpool, but although the two clubs were very close to becoming one, the negotiations held no such worries for the Seasiders who ran out comfortable winners against Rossendale with an entertaining 5–3 victory to maintain the pressure on the leaders, and it was Rossendale who were the next side to face Liverpool at Anfield on 23 March.

First was the small matter of hosting a Liverpool

Senior Cup tie against Chester. The visitors proved no match for a rampant Liverpool side who ran out comfortable winners by hitting four without reply to set up a tasty rematch with rivals Bootle with Cameron, Hugh McQueen, Miller and McVean all getting on the score sheet.

While the Liverpool Cup was an important trophy of its day, it is through league campaigns that the true worth of all teams must be judged. With all the sides at the summit dismissing all they met there was little between these three teams at the top of the table. And so it was with John McCartney not available that Wally Richardson took his place in the midfield to make his debut for Liverpool as they played their last home league game of the season. Liverpool got off to an unusually slow start before getting into their stride. Fortunately for them Rossendale could not convert their early superiority into goals as the Liverpool defence stood firm by whatever means possible. A lesser defence would surely have cracked as the visitors gave a very good account of themselves.

Matt McQueen was by now warming to his new role in goal and was credited with producing a number of fine saves in this opening onslaught. The fans, aware that this was possibly their last chance to see their idols at Anfield this season, and certainly the last time in the league, roused their team with their more vocal than usual support. Buoyed by this, the home side gradually played their way back into the game and made Rossendale pay for not converting their early chances when Smith steered McVean's pass into the net for the opening goal after some excellent work by Miller and McQue in the build up.

Their lead was short lived as Rossendale were soon back on level terms as the game flowed from end to end. A rare defensive error from the otherwise dependable McLean gave Matt McQueen no chance as Rossendale equalised from close range. It was clear that Liverpool wanted to end their final home game of the season on a high and after the break they managed to get a winner to keep them in first place. Hugh McQueen sent in one of his trademark corners into the box and McVean rose high above the defence to nod the ball into the net. The win was vital as Bury stayed in second with a four goal demolition of South Shore and Blackpool left Higher Walton propping up the division by hitting five goals without reply past their leaky defence that had now conceded a mighty 104 goals to stay just behind them. The pressure was mounting on all three clubs at the top of the division as this exciting season was now drawing to close. Liverpool had to wait another two weeks before they could play their final fixture of the season while the teams around them caught up on their games in hand. Bury had two games less than the leaders while Blackpool, although they had four matches to catch up, the club were distracted as talks about the merger with South Shore were now well advanced.

And so it was on 15 April that Liverpool played out their final game of their first season with a trip to Southport Central. This was do-or-die with regard to their title hopes. The start of the game was delayed as the referee had not turned up and after a considerable delay it was agreed by both teams that a local man from the crowd with previous experience was allowed to officiate the match as the light was fading fast and this was long before the introduction of floodlights. The match started 40 minutes late and for the home side it was worth waiting for as they took the lead after just 12 minutes when W. Hastings headed home from a corner.

The lead only lasted eight minutes as Miller was on hand to even things up before the break in a game Liverpool could not afford to lose. With so much at stake it was not a great surprise that quality suffered in this nervy affair and the result was that the pair cancelled each other out with neither side able to score again in the game and it ended with them both sharing a point each and left Liverpool with a nervous wait to see how their rivals got on.

Fortunately for Liverpool Blackpool could only manage the same score in their game against local rivals Fleetwood. Their match ended in disgraceful scenes as a fight broke out towards the end of their bad tempered game. A brawl between two of the players resulted in the crowd running onto the pitch to separate them. A rumour soon circulated that one of the Blackpool strikers had been beaten up quite badly by a group of Fleetwood fans and was hospitalised after being carried off the pitch in a state of unconsciousness. The report turned out to be utterly false and the matter was only resolved at a public meeting in the town hall a few days later in a bid to quell the rising anger fuelled by false rumours and speculation as the authorities feared substantial public unrest.

What was utterly undeniable was Liverpool now faced an anxious wait as the result meant that they were joined at the top of the table on 36 points by Blackpool with Bury two more behind. What made things so unbearable was that both their rivals still had a game left to play and McKenna's men could only sit back and watch as they played out their final games of the season.

The title was Blackpool's to lose as they were finishing the campaign strongly with a 6–1 thumping of bottom side Higher Walton even though the visitors, who were nailed on to finish with the wooden spoon, scored first and held the 1–0 lead over the Seasiders at half-time. Now tied on points at the top, Blackpool faced the same Southport Central side that Liverpool had recently drawn with at Scarisbrick New Road. The signs were not good for Liverpool as Central had lost 13 of their 21 games that season and, although they were much improved in recent months, they were expected to add another notch to that total against column against in-form Blackpool. But, as many seasoned punters will testify, the form book is not always a perfect guide to results.

Central won the toss and never looked back. W. Hastings scored the only goal of the match in the first half as Blackpool failed at the last. The Central lads gave as good as they got as the Blackpool players choked when it mattered. A shock 1–0 defeat meant they ended the season on the same points as Liverpool, but with a superior goal difference. The title, though, went to Anfield as positions in the league at this time were decided by the peculiar method of a goal average in which the amount of goals scored is divided by the amount they have conceded over the season to give a goal average. Blackpool did not come out favourably in this method, despite having scored 82 goals to Liverpool's 66, the fact they conceded 31 times to their rival's 19 meant the sums added up to Liverpool having a goal average of 3.4 to Blackpool's 2.6. Liverpool's mean defence played a massive part in their winning of the Lancashire League in their first attempt. A feat made all the more remarkable by the fact they lost their goalkeeper, Sydney Ross, in the run in who was never to play again.

A delighted John Houlding received the trophy from the league at his headquarters in the Sandon Hotel in front of a jubilant team. One of the delights of having a brewer as a chairman and being able to use his hotel for a celebratory party must be a free bar. But although the Lancashire League trophy was now secured and safely in the trophy cabinet, and undoubtedly these were heady times at the club indeed, the champagne was put on ice as there was still the small matter of the Liverpool Cup to be decided.

A semi-final against Bootle was on the cards just two days after their final league game so there was no chance to celebrate, although there was something of a party atmosphere when the two met at Anfield on the following Monday. Both sides had met since their Lancashire Cup tie on 11 March that ended the promising career of Sydney Ross when, two weeks later, they played a benefit match for Bootle's Dannie Kirkwood, a former Everton winger while they played at Anfield, who broke his leg against South Shore in November of the previous year. McOwen made an appearance in goal as McKenna put out his strongest possible side. This was a must-win game for Liverpool, not only for reasons of revenge following their last encounter, but also because Everton were awaiting the winners. This was a rare opportunity that neither Houlding nor McKenna would want to miss.

For such a big game the fact that only 5,000

turned up and paid up their hard earned cash to watch the match at Anfield was a disappointment. The visitors won the toss and chose to have the wind at their backs in the first half so the honour of kicking off fell to McVean. The game was barely five minutes old when McOwen was beaten after Bootle broke away on a counter-attack and put the ball in the back of the net. To the great relief of the Liverpool players, who had yet to really get going, the referee ruled the goal out for offside.

This shock was just what McKenna's men needed and, with Hannah reminding them all of the prize awaiting them in his usual no-nonsense manner, they soon got down to playing the football that had won them so many admirers throughout the season. The Bootle players were now very much second best and could not match the desire shown by the Liverpool players who, to a man, out-fought their opposite numbers. They were rewarded with a goal from the irrepressible Miller. The striker ended another of his winding runs by rounding the veteran J. Jackson in the Bootle goal before side-footing the ball into the net. Now with their noses in front there was no way the Liverpool lads were going to let this one slip. They had become quite adept at defending early leads as the season wore on and made Bootle expend their energy in fruitlessly chasing the ball around the pitch in an effort to get back into the game. So it was that Miller's strike proved to be the difference between the two sides on the day and Liverpool were safely through to the final.

The chance for Houlding and McKenna to face Everton so soon was the stuff of dreams. All season they had been subjected to abuse from the pro-Everton sections of the press and the city. They had been written off by some as no-hopers that would never rise to the dizzy heights of an Everton side that had just lost the FA Cup final to Wolves and became the first side to be awarded runners-up medals following their 1–0 defeat. It took them three attempts to overcome a magnificent Preston North End side after the first two semi-final ties ended in stalemate. This was the first time that the final was to be decided outside of London as the pair met in Fallowfield, Manchester. Goodison Park was to host the final a year later before it again returned to London where the grand old competition would be decided for over a century with just the one final at Old Trafford in 1915 when Sheffield United beat Chelsea 3–0.

The first derby between Everton and Liverpool took place on 22 April 1893 in front of 10,000 people on Bootle's ground for reasons of neutrality, with just as many locked outside such was the interest in this game. First division Everton was, of course, considered more likely to win, but president Houlding was determined to show his old team the might of his new one. Herbie Arthur, from Blackburn and a former player for Rovers, had been handed the difficult job of refereeing the match.

All week there had been feverish talk about what teams the two clubs would put out to represent them in a game dripping with sub plots and intrigue. As it was, Everton did not play their strongest side for this game as the executive had organised a friendly match against Renton on the same day. The reasons behind this are not known, speculation at the time varied between their fear of losing with a full strength side would have been too much to handle and others who thought them so dismissive of

Liverpool that they thought them a walk over. The line-up did feature three first team players, including the goalkeeper Williams, and therefore was still a strong enough side to beat most teams. If the motivation for their hastily organised game against Renton was a financial one then it backfired on the club because that game was poorly attended and one newspaper hack at the time believed there to be more Everton fans locked out of this game than attended the one against the talented Scots.

With the talking over, Miller started the match in brilliant sunshine and predictably the players did not give an inch from the beginning as the battle quickly became quite heated. The ref had to have a stern word with Joe McQue for being too enthusiastic in the opening minutes. The midfielder was a squat and powerful man famed for his hard tackling, but his love for the rougher aspects of the game belied his eye for important goals. McQue had played been picked up by McKenna after impressing as a reserve at Celtic and made an instant impact with the fans with his two goals in the first league match against Higher Walton all those months ago. He would go on to play almost 150 games for Liverpool, scoring 14 times during his spell at the club, but it was as a defensive midfielder that McQue was to make his name and it was not unusual for him to be spoken to so early in a game.

With the Scot now dictating the game from the centre of the park, Liverpool put their opponents under severe pressure and Everton would have had no complaints about being behind early on in the match as they failed to get going initially. Williams was forced to pull off an excellent save to deny Matt McQueen after five minutes when he tipped his powerful drive over the bar. Wylie and Miller looked in dangerous form in the opening minutes as they combined expertly. The pair were taking delight in exchanging passes between each other with such precision that the Everton players looked like dogs chasing a balloon. Their excellent build up play fashioned an opening for McBride just inside the box and the former Renton man's well-struck shot cannoned back off the bar and was thumped clear, as was an effort from Matt McQueen just minutes later.

Liverpool eventually took a deserved lead roughly 30 minutes into the game and to add insult to injury it was former Toffee, Tom Wylie, who scored with a superbly struck effort that fizzed hard and low past Williams in the Everton goal and would have beaten any goalkeeper in the country. If the game was fast before, it was now played at light speed as both sides got stuck in. McLean and Hannah were involved in running battles with the Everton forwards as the game threatened to turn ugly while McQue was again given a finger wagging lecture by the referee for hauling and brawling in the midfield. To their credit the Everton lads did not take conceding a goal lightly and fought back bravely, but they were no match for the muscular Scots in either brains or brawn. Things looked to have got significantly worse for Everton just before the break when the ball was again in the back of their net from a Matt McQueen corner, but the referee ruled that it had not hit anyone on the way and gave a goal kick. A corner was seen as an indirect free-kick until 1924 and the goal, although legal today, did not stand. So it was that the feisty first half ended 1–0 to Liverpool with Houlding and McKenna's men having by far the better of the first half.

The referee extended the half-time break because of the exertions of the players in the hot sun. The second half was a much more even affair as both sides traded chances. Everton came close to equalising soon after the break when Hannah and McOwen combined on the line to deny Gordon from a well taken free-kick.

Both McQueens had chances denied for Liverpool while Wylie was denied by a magnificent save from Williams when everyone thought he had beaten the keeper with a curling shot midway through the second half as the thrilling game flowed from end to end. The drama reached fever pitch in the final minute as the match ended in controversial circumstances.

With just seconds left on the clock Everton attacked and were awarded a corner when McOwen pushed the ball around his post. As the ball was swung in it was met by the head of one of the Everton strikers and looked to be heading towards the back of the net when it was clawed off the line by a hand. The Everton players claimed it was a Liverpool defender that had fisted the ball away in the penalty area, but in the melee it was difficult to tell. The ref could not say for definite who the hand belonged to and all the players surrounded and jostled him while trying to put their cases for and against the penalty claim. Mr Arthur had no choice but to consult his linesman, who was also an FA appointed official and completely neutral as competition rules demanded, in a bid to get to the bottom of the argument as the Liverpool fans held their breath. A referee cannot give what he has not seen so he decided the fairest way to decide this was to have a drop-ball in the box and the rarest of tussles ensued with a full 20 men piling in to contest it. In a situation like this it is good to have men of iron will and determination in your side and it was no real surprise when Joe McQue, the hard man's hard man, somehow emerged from the scrum with the ball at his feet and smacked it a full 40 yards up the pitch as the final whistle went.

Despite this controversial ending Liverpool were 'either equal or superior in every department' in this historical game. The *Liverpool Mercury* reported:

> McOwen in goal did all that was required of him in a confident manner. Hannah and McLean gave a splendid exhibition of defence, and neither seemed bothered much by the Everton attackers, their kicking being strong and well directed all through. The half-back line was perhaps the rock upon which Everton stranded. McQue at centre was happy in the extreme, and completely spoilt Hartley, the work of McCartney and McBride being almost as good. With the half-backs so much in evidence the Liverpool forwards had plenty of opportunities of showing their capabilities, and they did it in a pleasing way. They displayed no selfishness, and taking and parting with the ball in no halting fashion were very speedy. The pace was remarkable, and that it should be sustained as it was on such a warm day was evidence that Liverpool were in good condition.

Everton protested against the result with William Clayton lodging an official complaint about 'the general incompetence of the referee'. This looked to be a case of sour grapes on the face of it because of the way the final ended and the specific matter of who handled the ball. The more vague plea of general incompetence was the only one that the FA would have listened to rather than the specific one of whether it was McOwen, McLean or Matt

McQueen that punched the ball clear. If their charge was just a ploy to stop Houlding being presented with the trophy then it worked as the FA had no choice but to investigate the claims. Liverpool themselves could have complained about the fact that the corner should never have been taken in the first place because the full 90 minutes had long since passed, but again Houlding kept a dignified silence on this and patiently awaited the outcome.

Not surprisingly the Everton protest came to nothing and the Liverpool captain, Andrew Hannah was presented with the trophy by Mr A. Bull to round off a stunning first season by the club. Perhaps if Everton had played their strongest team in the first place then they would have had more sympathy from the organisers of the competition. Liverpool had won the Lancashire League and the Liverpool Senior Cup in the club's inaugural season. The reserves finished top of their league making it an impressive hat-trick of trophies for the club that would go on to make winning a habit and become one of the most successful sides in the country. Later both cups were stolen from a local pawnbrokers that belonged to a fellow director at the club where they were being kept so they could be put safely on display in the window for all to see and the club had to pay £130 to replace them. This was just the start of the colourful history of Liverpool Football Club. The *Daily News* of 4 September 1893 reported:

> Friday night the two silver challenge cups which were won by the Liverpool Football Club last season, viz., Liverpool & District Cup and Lancashire League Cup, were stolen by burglars from the pawnshop of Mr Charles Gibson, Paddington, Liverpool, where they were on view. The burglars forced open the door of the shop with a jemmy, and took away the

prizes, which are of considerable value. So far the police have failed to obtain a clue to the missing cups.

With the club now well and truly established and some shiny silverware tucked away in the trophy cabinet the first season could only be seen as a remarkable success by Houlding and his team of all the Macs. The impressive Anfield once again had a team fit to grace it and one the fans could be proud of. The squad remained much the same for the next season with the tragic omission of Ross who never fully recovered from the blow to the head he suffered against Bootle.

The Liverpool board had proved themselves to an ambitious bunch in the past but following the successful season there were now a few within the club that believed they were obligated to defend their title and not look towards league football. What was soon to follow in great piece of opportunism by the wily McKenna. Harry Lockett was the former Stoke City manager and was now sharing that role with the job of being the league's first secretary. He was later to resign his post at Stoke so he could concentrate on his administrative role which was growing more demanding year on year. An advert was put out in the summer of 1893 by Lockett asking for clubs to apply for entry into the second division. McKenna spotted it and sent a telegram in reply stating the intent of Liverpool to join despite having no authority to do so and without consulting the board. His job at the club was to deal with the players while Barclay looked after such details as secretary. He signed off the telegram with Barclay's name and sent it nonetheless. Some hours later he was summoned by a confused Barclay who had in his hand a reply from the league informing Liverpool their application had been successful and that an official was to report to a meeting at 3pm the next day in London to argue the case for their election to the league and if they were successful to also arrange fixtures. Some stern words followed amongst the board as many were happy to consolidate with another season in the Lancashire League while some believed the club should move onwards in a bid to become bigger than Everton. McKenna argued his point skilfully and eventually persuaded the other members to allow him to travel south the next day for the meeting.

There were two spaces left in the league being chased by five clubs. The four others were Woolwich Arsenal (later to become Arsenal after they were moved from their original home in south London to Highbury across the river), Doncaster Rovers, Loughborough and Middlesbrough Ironopolis (not to be confused with the Middlesbrough side of today). Arsenal were elected unanimously into the league as a reward for the way they had embraced professionalism in the face of fierce opposition in the south. The country was still divided in terms of allowing the players to make a living from the sport. Arsenal were pretty much a lone voice in the capital with regard to the promotion of professionalism and were shunned by most other clubs around them. Their stance earned them great sympathy within the league committee for the way they were popularising the sport in the south and although their inclusion would increase the amount of travelling for everyone in the league it was thought that the increased gates by the visits of the Northern giants would more than compensate the sides.

Liverpool faced a tougher fight and it was touch and go as to whether they or Ironopolis would be voted into the second division. The clincher for McKenna and Liverpool was the magnificent stadium they had in Anfield as well as the ever increasing crowds. The sport was growing faster in Liverpool than anywhere else.

It was to be the first of many league meetings for McKenna as his future was to lay in football administration. While continuing in various roles at Liverpool Football Club throughout his life, his concern for the welfare of the poor of Liverpool during his 35 years with the West Derby Union and his love of fairness extended into the football world. McKenna was elected to the Football League's management committee in 1902 as the Football League was now based in Preston at this time.

As McKenna flourished within his administrative role, so did Liverpool. The Irishman had to surrender his role in team affairs, but remained on the board of the club. He appointed the knowledgeable Tom Watson as his successor in 1896. Watson had twice won the league with Sunderland after guiding them from obscurity and was to deliver the title for Liverpool just five years after joining.

Football in general continued to grow under his stewardship and McKenna became a fierce critic of the maximum wage system. His belief was the club could quite easily afford to pay their players well through decent wages or a lucrative bonus scheme. Around this time there are reports of Liverpool players earning as much as £10 a week while most others in the division were on around £4. Money and players wages was as hot a topic a hundred years ago as it is now. Within six years he became a vice-president and then league president two years later, an unpaid position he was to hold for over two decades until his death some 26 years later.

By the time he took over the role of president in 1910 he had gained the nickname 'honest John'. His work brought him into contact with rich and poor alike and crossed the class system. He treated everyone the same and this made him a very popular figure. 'Neither blowing hot nor cold, he preserves the even tenor of his course,' was how one of his contemporaries described him.

He also wanted to look after injured players because he was aware that they, like sick people in other walks of life, still had families to feed and we must bear in mind this was before the great welfare state we all take for granted today. On his watch the players union, the PFA, was formed largely through his influence. That is not to say he was the instigator. That honour belongs to Billy Meridith and a select group of strong minded players. At first there was a lot of opposition to the PFA from the powers that be in football, but McKenna oversaw the negotiations— in his view it was a kind of necessary evil in that it took control away from the central committee, but did benefit the players.

When professionalism was introduced into the game, Everton, through McKenna's influence, were one of the first clubs to totally embrace it. The club and the board at the time saw the benefits to all concerned that running a club in a business like manner could bring. And by all concerned I mean players, fans and shareholders alike. He also oversaw the massive expansion of the league from 24 teams in two divisions into the format we know today with the huge football pyramid. The explosion in the popularity of football was breathtaking as in 1875, it was still largely a game for the leisured elite, but by the start of the First World War it had been embraced as the national sport and was very much at the heart of much English male culture. Upon McKenna's insistence a central fund was set up in which the richer clubs would contribute to assist with financial aid to the clubs who were losing out because of the move away from a system where all gates were pooled and shared out. He also introduced the payment of 20% of home gate receipts to be given to the away side so there was still some sort of distribution of wealth from the bigger clubs to the smaller ones. Such was the success of the league under his tenure that many other countries looked to the English model as a blueprint for their own as professional football spread around the world. He was presented with no less than five long service medals by the league, although he admitted later on that the medal he was most proud of was his long service medal from his regiment. McKenna was not a man for a fuss to be made over him.

In addition to all of this, he had two spells as Liverpool chairman; 1909–1914 and 1917–1919 as well as being director at the club for a number of years and served on the Lancashire FA, the FA Council and the management committee. He was without doubt one of the great early administrators of the English game, a man who was widely admired, respected and occasionally feared and one who had a major influence on the early days of the sport.

While on official business in 1936 he fell desperately ill having been to Inverness to watch Scotland amateurs face England amateurs. He hid the extent of the illness from those around him as was his custom. Soon after, he was at a league meeting in Manchester in which he persuaded the committee to wage war on the new fangled method of gambling called the 'football pools'. He was uncomfortable with betting on matches in case it led to games being rigged in a bid to make money. Following this meeting he had an accident. McKenna lived his life in a small house near Anfield and was on his way to catch his train back to Liverpool when he slipped and fell at the train station. Sadly, his injuries affected him greatly. Just two weeks later McKenna passed away peacefully on 22 March 1936 at Walton hospital in Liverpool.

There is heavy irony in the fact that it was in Scotland that he fell ill as it was here that he first made his name in the sport that he loved and dedicated so much of his life with his shrewd recruitment drive that formed the backbone of the first Liverpool team. His great friend John Houlding oversaw the growth of the club and was himself appointed as Lord Mayor of Liverpool in 1897. By the time of his death in 1902, still unable to clear his name with the Everton board who cruelly campaigned against him during the split, he took comfort in the fact he had seen the Liverpool team he started all those years before crowned champions and converted to wearing the famous blood red shirts we know today. The foundations for the club had been laid though and his portrait now hangs in Goodison Park as the club acknowledged their debt to this pioneer of Merseyside football who, along with McKenna oversaw football's first foreign invasion when they set up what was to become one of the biggest teams in world football today with 'the Team of all the Macs'.